D0389741

"Brands need to be backed by accountable, reachable people inside businesses (not websites, and interminable electronic answering systems). The way to customer loyalty is not necessarily the brand, but the business behind the brand. How that business acts and reacts, how it deals with relationships, how it deals with complaints and problems, and above all how it interfaces with customers and consumers is the essence of marketing. The worry is, many businesses seem to adopt a different negative strategy. In this sense, political marketing can be the ultimate example of short-term hype and glossy promises, exchanged for votes; and then – post-election – consumers (née voters) are forgotten ... until the next time! And in 2007, there are many examples of poor, inappropriate, and even Machiavellian marketing than ever before. When this is coupled with declining levels of customer satisfaction, and all the evidence pointing to a downward trend, customers and their needs need to be elevated to center stage if we're ever to stop and reverse the slide.

In this challenging and engaging new book, Ian Buckingham puts these factors in stark relief, demanding the attention of senior executives, line managers, consumers and employees alike."

Philip J. Kitchen
Professor of Strategic Marketing
Director, Research Centre for Marketing, Communications,
and International Strategy, University of Hull

BRAND ENGAGEMENT

How Employees Make or Break Brands

Ian P. Buckingham

© Ian Buckingham 2008

All rights reserved. No reproduction, copy or transmission of this publication may be made without written permission.

No paragraph of this publication may be reproduced, copied or transmitted save with written permission or in accordance with the provisions of the Copyright, Designs and Patents Act 1988, or under the terms of any licence permitting limited copying issued by the Copyright Licensing Agency, 90 Tottenham Court Road, London W1T 4LP.

Any person who does any unauthorised act in relation to this publication may be liable to criminal prosecution and civil claims for damages.

The author has asserted his right to be identified as the author of this work in accordance with the Copyright, Designs and Patents Act 1988.

First published 2008 by
PALGRAVE MACMILLAN
Houndmills, Basingstoke, Hampshire RG21 6XS and
175 Fifth Avenue, New York, N.Y. 10010
Companies and representatives throughout the world

PALGRAVE MACMILLAN is the global academic imprint of the Palgrave Macmillan division of St. Martin's Press, LLC and of Palgrave Macmillan Ltd. Macmillan® is a registered trademark in the United States, United Kingdom and other countries. Palgrave is a registered trademark in the European Union and other countries.

ISBN-13: 978–0–230–57306–2
ISBN-10: 0–230–57306–1

This book is printed on paper suitable for recycling and made from fully managed and sustained forest sources. Logging, pulping and manufacturing processes are expected to conform to the environmental regulations of the country of origin.

A catalogue record for this book is available from the British Library.

A catalog record for this book is available from the Library of Congress.

10 9 8 7 6 5 4 3 2 1
17 16 15 14 13 12 11 10 09 08

Printed and bound in Great Britain by
Cromwell Press Ltd, Trowbridge, Wiltshire

This is for Lisa, Jack, Holly and Alice

CONTENTS

LIST OF FIGURES AND TABLES

Figures

Table

ACKNOWLEDGEMENTS

This project has taken a lot of hard work. It started with a promise to myself and it's important to me to thank everyone who has made a contribution toward the fulfilment of that promise. I appreciate the influence that clients, colleagues and partners past and present have had on the development of many of the core themes and concepts. Despite the fact that many management texts may fail to acknowledge it, this type of book can be nothing other than a collaboration. It represents the evolution of thinking honed by experience and has therefore involved a significant cast of characters. Whether provocateurs, conspirators or catalysts I'm sure you know who you are but I would like to single out the following people for a special mention:

Caroline Hempstead; Wendy Russell; Mandy Thatcher; Phillip Kitchen; Ramesh Thomas; Tim Bulmer; Bill Parsons; Summer Fern; Anne Downey; Barbara Hannant; Phil Morley; Debby DeFranco; John Smythe; Dennis MacDonald; Emma Snyder; David Broome; Stephen Rutt and the Palgrave Macmillan team and all at Aardvark Editorial.

In addition, thank you to all of the threshold guardians who gave permission for the use of the quotes and references which have helped to bring the book to life.

Most importantly, I'm extremely grateful for the support provided by my business partners and muses Paul and Lisa. Your encouragement and nurturing has been invaluable.

The author and publishers would like to thank Robert A. Cooke and J. Clayton Lafferty, Organizational Culture Inventory, Human Synergistics International, for Figures 4.3, 4.4 and 4.5. Copyright © 1987–2007. All rights reserved. Used by permission. Human Synergistics® and Organizational Culture Inventory® are registered trademarks of Human Synergistics International, Plymouth, MI, U.S.A.

Every effort has been made to trace all the copyright holders but if any have been inadvertently overlooked the publishers will be pleased to make the necessary arrangements at the first opportunity.

… I'd raise up an effigy of the term "internal brand alignment" and burn it. (Buckingham, 2003)

PROLOGUE

BRAND ENGAGEMENT
IN CONTEXT

Capitalism and consumerism are two sides of the same coin. Brand management and capitalism go hand in hand. So when arguably the preeminent anti-establishment establishment figure in one of the leading world economies links capitalism, consumerism, and global warming, it's time brand managers sat up and listened. In an interview with the *Observer* (April 8, 2007), Sir Jonathon Porritt said:

> I think capitalism is patently unable to go on growing the size of the consumer economy for any more people in the world today because the levels of consumption are already undermining life support systems on which we depend. We've got to rethink the basic premise behind capitalism.

Very strong words from the former director of Friends of the Earth and now chairman of the UK government's Sustainable Development Commission. Depending on how you look at it, in what I believe has been hailed by Tom Peters, amongst other notable management gurus and commentators, as the century of the brand, brands certainly have the power to influence the globe for better, or worse.

While necessarily ambitious in terms of reach, you'll be glad to hear that this book isn't another apocalyptic treatise railing at the evils of capitalism and brand imperialism from the comfort of the green band-wagon. I've worked in hard-nosed business for a long time and certainly believe in making money. What follows is a critical examination of the vital, evolving function of brands but also of the people-centered success factors that contribute to effective brand management.

I do believe strongly in the power of brands. I also believe, however, that they can and should be leveraged to enrich and fulfill the lives of all stakeholders – certainly if any brand is to have a positive and lasting legacy. In short, there's a very clear business case for engaging employees with brands, which has implications far outweighing mere commercial imperative. Sadly, at the moment, not everyone can see it.

A recent study of customer experiences (Mumford, 2007) by YouGov plc, the analysts who use funky social networking methodologies and, as a result of their people panel approach, claim to have their finger constantly on the nation's pulse, suggests that the general public is growing increasingly intolerant of poor customer experiences. At last.

The study reveals that British consumers complain up to five times a year. Of the 2,800 British consumers polled, 69 percent had complained to a company and more than three-quarters (79 percent) of these stated that they had complained about their treatment between one and five times in the past 12 months.

I work across a host of industries as a consultant and am aware that my personal circumstances mean that I fit the customer demographic to which many suppliers aspire. I am firmly of the view that there is a worrying trend – general customer service levels are undoubtedly on the wane. In addition, there is a clear discrepancy when it comes to the resolution of customer complaints (and customer service lore from the 1980s teaches us that problems are opportunities, if handled properly). Sixty percent of Britons expect a problem to be fixed to their satisfaction, but only 27 percent report that this is the case. Disturbingly, 34 percent of respondents state that companies did nothing once a complaint had been made. Clearly, the customer doesn't always come first, as it appears that many suppliers are playing with acceptable nonconformance levels, permissible tolerances, and are literally banking on inertia.

Certainly, the barometer has shifted further toward realistic rather than melodramatic when I say that, in many sectors, we do appear to be on the edge of a lofty precipice staring down at an imminent customer service catastrophe. When consumer goods are cheaper now than in the 1990s yet people in their twenties and thirties can't afford a house, and when the price of basic cotton romper suits, for example, makes it more cost-effective to throw them away when soiled rather than wash and reuse them, then consumerism has clearly gone mad. In this respect, I do agree with Porritt's sentiment that "there's an awful lot of unnecessary consumption, conspicuous consumption, irresponsible consumption" – but is it making people happy?

Rather than blame consumerism and, by implication, brands for the fact that our planet is about to "pop," I suggest that the answers lie within the very makeup of the selfsame free-market economy which Porritt lambasts. Free will got us here, education liberates us, so free will should get us out. The answer to effective brand management doesn't just mean better design, it lies in authentic brand engagement, and the key to brand engagement lies in exercising and encouraging the responsible and seductive free will we've all grown accustomed to. It's all a matter of motive and focus.

Brands are undoubtedly powerful. The turnover of many branded corporations (and sometimes branded individuals) outstrips the GDP of several countries. Wal-Mart, for example, which allegedly turns over in excess of $1 billion a day, is apparently the largest company ever to have existed and can, arguably, have a greater impact on the US economy and therefore the world economy than any other US institution. But Wal-Mart certainly didn't ask for that level of social responsibility and its directors will doubtless be conscious of its growing weight.

As the saying goes, power can corrupt, and as professionals and as consumers I believe that we've been dazzled by the material manifestations of brands for too long. I believe that, both within businesses, as employers and employees, and as consumers (guises we all don throughout our lives), we often forget that brands are far more than the sum of their trappings. Having been seduced by and having fallen in love with conspicuous consumption, however, we've lost touch with the higher order values that brands should cater for. We're stuck in a cycle of superficial one-night stands at the expense of nurturing relationships. It's time we all joined the authenticity underground, the great brand revolution.

But first we have to admit that, in terms of our relationship with brands, we really are missing the point. Great brands aren't just about design, advertising, "smoke and mirrors," promises about a life we don't have. Brands are fundamentally about people and relationships, about culture, about fulfillment, and the best brands appeal to higher order values we all possess, somewhere. And they make money doing it.

Brands are nothing if they aren't about behaviors, just as promises become lies if they aren't followed through. The secret is to encourage appropriate behaviors that reinforce long-term survival and the constructive evolution of the many rather than a short-term fix for the privileged few.

Too many companies are failing to recognize that brands should be about the promise keepers not the promise makers, the staff not the logos, customer satisfaction not advertising awards, sustainability not just share price. As a result, not only are many brands acting irresponsibly, they're missing a commercial opportunity – the search for higher order fulfillment that is the more mature phase in the development of any culture, once the baser consumer needs have been met.

Wasn't it that noted but ultimately tragic aristocrat of personal brand development, Oscar Wilde, who said that "illusion is the first of all pleasures"? But as consumers, employees, employers, and even as citizens (to use a loaded phrase), we have good reasons to wise up and recognize the difference between illusion and delusion. From the newspapers we buy, to the sporting teams we support (on the back page) or the ideologies we sympathize with (on the front), brand think plays a clear, although sometimes clandestine role in the decisions we make.

At a level down, the selfsame newspapers are also full of contradictions between record bonus payouts to a very small number of people, contrasted with soaring levels of employee turnover and complaints to customer ombudsmen. Despite consuming more products than at any time in our evolution, customers are becoming increasingly disgruntled and, most importantly, so are employees. Clearly something in the great brand hunt isn't working. Make the link between the pages and it's clear to see that brands do have an undoubted social power and implicit social responsibility.

So why are so many of us still complicit in this self-deluding conspiracy? When we feel let down by the brands we give our commitment to, it's usually because they, in turn, are letting down their own people. There are just too many stories emerging about employees being forgotten at bonus time and yet being invited to values-cascade launch parties on the same day, or of customers being blatantly misled. Perhaps if we can bridge the gap between brand awareness and social consciousness, we might all feel a whole lot better. And there really is a clear business case for it that doesn't feature a heart or a single flower.

I like to think that, rather unexceptionally, I've led a relatively well-rounded life to date. While building a career in business and consultancy, I've embraced the arts, sampled many of the finer things, traveled, started a family, and have immersed myself in culture as well as enjoying team and individual sports. Most importantly, I've steadfastly refused to pull down the shutters between the business and home worlds. It's little surprise to me that an eclectic mix of mavericks ranging from John Lennon, Confucius and John Maynard Keynes have been credited with saying words to the effect of "find a job you love and you'll never work another day in your life," as this remains a core ambition for most of us.

But the many parallels between the so-called business and leisure worlds are clearly being obscured. Somehow we're supposed to belong in one camp or the other, giving rise to contradictory terms like "arts in business" and "work/life balance." We're happy to listen to so-called motivational speakers from the leisure world or buy in theatrical companies to add magic dust to events, but primarily as corporate catharsis, big bangs to make a point over dinner, act as a catalyst and then disappear; not an end in themselves, not a means of permanently changing the way we interact, but a fleeting distraction. I believe that the same cultural schizophrenia applies to the world of brand management and the answer to the riddle of how to bring brands to life lies in the alleviation of this condition.

I'm going to unashamedly use a sporting cliché to sum up the importance of employee engagement to 21st-century business: "the manager won the league because he had the full support of the dressing room." Apply this analogy to any business and it stands to reason that the modern manager who fails to engage with the people who are expected to keep the promises made to customers is ultimately doomed to failure. Multiply this by the ripple effect of layers of management and you can chart the half-life of a brand.

It's well known that Sir Clive Woodward, former coach of the England rugby team, World Cup winners who dominated world rugby for a number of years, attributes much of the success of his team to leadership principles honed off the field as a successful businessman and his book *Winning* (2005) successfully explains his belief in blending business and sporting methodology. Woodward is lauded for his belief in professional, values-based communication, informed by and informing the team brand, creating a performance culture, and inspiring the winning individuals who make up the team. Whether he is working as head of his company or sports team makes no difference. Woodward's philosophy transcends sport, just as the wisdom of Ali transcends boxing or the iconic music and imagery associated with Miles Davis has come to mean so much to style aficionados and rebels alike. If their heroes bestride genres, doesn't it stand to reason that employees are more likely to be more effectively engaged if we stop trying to align and compartmentalize them and try to connect with them in a holistic way?

High-performing teams rely on great communication between the members of the wider team, including the management team. In the corporate world, internal communication, however, has historically been taken for granted. Virtually every day I hear a beleaguered manager cry: "but we all communicate – it's easy, it comes naturally, what's there to learn?" Until relatively recently, internal communication was dismissed as a shoddy outpost of HR or PR or the poor relation of marketing fed from the scraps of the customer communication budget when someone near the seat of power bothered to let the staff know about a development or a change. How the communication worm has turned.

Back in 2000, while leading a team within the Omnicom fold, I participated in an international, pan-industry survey (Smythe Dorward Lambert, 2000) of largely blue-chip senior executives. We found that roughly one-third had no dedicated internal communication resource above junior management level and only about one in ten had regular access to the boardroom. Having since completed a similar exercise including nearly 2,000 individuals from over 300 similar organizations, we found that, by 2005, 83 percent had a dedicated and specialist internal communications function, the vast majority of whom had regular board access in one form or another.

This dramatic professionalization of internal communication has certainly increased tensions between the external-facing communication disciplines and their peers who serve the internal market, but it isn't the only factor behind successful and lasting brands. The core purpose of this book is to illustrate, with a mixture of storytelling, theory, and case studies, how brands come to life from the inside and how authentic engagement with employees, developed from the ground up rather than cascaded, creates strong and lasting brands.

This isn't a one-eyed, revisionist attempt to reempower HR and what some see as the "touchy-feely" brigade of introspective bleeding hearts. It's a pragmatic exploration of the power of employee engagement, regardless of whose responsibility it is and how a people-centered approach to leadership impacts where it counts, on the bottom line. Throughout the book, I put forward a strong argument for partnership in the delivery of communication as the most effective way of managing the most powerful manifestation of what organizations represent – the brand.

This book tells a story spanning two decades of consultancy and calls upon a cast of characters drawn from a wide array of industries and organizations.

This is neither a star chamber heralding the usual suspects nor is it a rogues' gallery of horror stories (all the case studies have been carefully selected to be pragmatic and accessible rather than intimidating). It's an honest and open journey that charts the evolution of employee engagement as one of the most powerful forces behind the alternate realities of commercial success or creeping brand death. Unlike a number of management tomes, I can personally verify the contents, having worked firsthand with each of the contributors at some point and having stuck around for the results.

While this work represents the chorus of voices reflecting the thoughts, feelings, and wise counsel of many peers, colleagues, and clients down the years, the story is told primarily from two perspectives. First and foremost, there is the first-person narrative of Everyman, the hero of the journey, who is both a classic literary device and the spokesperson for the common man. Second, there is the narrative voice of the trusted adviser, the observer charting the journey and signposting key messages.

I hope that somewhere along the journey you find something to interest you, a little entertainment, a measure of catharsis, and even a spark to light up an idea or two to help face the threats and opportunities of daily business life. Most of all, I hope it makes you look at brands from a different perspective and recognize their true potential – an ambition that I believe is very much in all our interests.

REFLECTIONS AND ACTIONS SHEET

(Why not use this page to record thoughts or ideas as you go?)

ACT 1

BRAND ENGAGEMENT, EVERYMAN AND THE DEATH OF THE HERO LEADER

Everyman is on his way to work on the 7.30 a.m. commuter train. He's rereading George Orwell's *Keep the Aspidistra Flying*, in between elbows, coughs, sneezes, and newspapers. The banality of its antihero Gordon Comstock, who resigned from his job with a lucrative advertising agency in favor of the life of a penniless poet, to romantically rage against Mammon, seems so childishly idealistic. How society has advanced since Orwell's pessimism between the wars. Looking around the smart suits in his carriage and out of the windows at the houses flashing by, he reflects on how he and his partner, like so many of his traveling peers, have made it onto the property ladder on the back of a free university degree, state welfare, and a job in the City with a generous pension package. They live at 8 New Road, a much-envied corner plot with solid middle-class neighbors; a teacher and his executive assistant wife. Nice couple. This is what his grandparents had suffered depression, conflict, and austerity for, the chance to create a landed generation of "baby boomers," who would, in due course, hand down the baton of middle-class affluence to their own lucky children.

Arriving at his office building, with its Palladian columns, exactly half an hour before his contracted start time, he is still, after all this time, a little intimidated by the cathedral-like dimensions of the entrance and halls, with the single arched window leading to the executive floor. A shadowy figure is looking down from the window as he arrives. Quickly passing the managerial suite, he is soon greeted by the usual chorus of affectionate banter. "Afternoon," calls one comedian. "Good, none of the managers have made it into our section yet," he thinks to himself. "I'll have enough time to grab a coffee before starting the recon-

11

ciliations and hopefully manage to get some real work done before the Monday meeting."

The ritual of Monday meetings seems to have been around forever. It is the organization's way of ensuring that key employees are aware of the changes to rules and regulations and standard procedures (copies available in the sequential instruction manuals controlled by the senior appointed officer), as well as any marketing initiatives that would inevitably mean additional work for frontline staff. The managers hate these sessions as much as the staff but go through the motions, managers at the front, officers arranged in rows in front of them. They always last for the first hour of the day, which means that many of Everyman's colleagues started early to ensure that their normal, time-critical tasks are finished first. Some had been at their desks since 6.30 a.m.

At the appointed time, they're summoned by the senior manager's assistant and take their places for the Monday briefing, ties straightened, notepads in hand, mouths shut and brains parked. The monolithic Georgian door slowly swings open.

WHAT DOES GREAT BRAND ENGAGEMENT FEEL LIKE?

Brand (noun or verb): torch, permanent mark deliberately made by hot iron, trade-mark goods, burn with hot iron (penally or to show ownership), impress on memory, stigmatize
Engage: bind by contract, bind by promise, hire, morally committed
Engagement: state of being engaged, moral commitment
Engaging: attractive, charming
SOURCE: *Concise Oxford Dictionary*

Branding is an overused and often poorly understood term. In a world where we should retain a healthy objectivity, it's often an enlightening and salutary exercise to track these seemingly modern "power" words back to their roots. Taking this back-to-basics approach, branding is reduced to little more than "making a mark signifying ownership." That's a loaded image in a contemporary context.

In the modern world of commerce, where services and experiences are traded as vociferously as physical goods and products, brands have come to signify a set of associations that we, as consumers and employees, make, linked to a set of communicated promises. In short, commercial brands are synonymous with promises.

12

Experiences are as distinct from services as services are from goods. (Pine and Gilmore, 1999)

So what is brand engagement?

Interestingly, the derivation of the word "engagement" evokes a form of emotional and moral commitment. To be engaged implies a condition or state of committed focus and that the state has been induced by an act of free will in response to seduction, attraction, or charm. Are we still talking about commerce here?

The most obvious use of the word "engagement" in society applies to the prenuptial promise made between two individuals committed to spend their lives together. It's another of what I call "power" words, a term reserved for our most important interactions; certainly not something that is easily earned or taken lightly.

An important distinction must be made between the terms "engagement" and "committed." The two are inextricably linked and yet true engagement, unlike contractual forms of commitment, is something that can't be legislated for, it really can't be driven, coerced, forced, or aligned; instead, it is reliant upon our higher order needs and depends upon the exercising of free will. Sure, we can be forced to focus on a presentation by peer pressure, obligation, seniority of the speaker, or responsibility. We can even be engrossed in an interesting television program or a compelling speech, but true engagement is of an altogether higher order and has a longevity all of its own.

Brand engagement describes the relationship between the promises made by an organization and the degree to which they connect with the needs-driven free will of individuals, be they employees or customers. It is the driving force behind decision making, relationships, and loyalty and is the single most important aspect of brand management. It's a vital step beyond compliance leading to true commitment and lasting commitment because it's self-determined.

When assisting the executive team behind the international Guinness brand to implement the next phase in its retail strategy, a number of my colleagues were asked to facilitate at a conference for the top 200 managers. As part of the briefing, we were told, in no uncertain terms, "not to make the same mistake the last lot did." Apparently, an agency had called upon the services of a well-known comedian to compere the event. Despite a briefing about the strong emotional ties between the people in the business and the brand, the comedian, apparently a lager drinker, made the ill-judged decision to ridicule their iconic dark stout. He was booed from the stage and was lucky to escape in one piece.

Tales of product-related brand loyalty abound. Sticking with the alcohol theme (often a subject to arouse strong emotions), I know of perfectly normal folk who, following the takeover of a local brewery and despite having frequented the same establishment for decades, traveled for miles to track down the last few kegs of pretakeover beer. Or consider the fanatics I refer to as "Macolytes." Simply utter the word "Apple" and it's like lighting a verbal fuse. Without any encouragement they volunteer the virtues of the superior Mac and passionately denounce the pragmatic population of PC users. They're more than champions; they love Macs and all things Apple and, as a result, they are probably Apple's most effective sales force. Chances are you know plenty of these folk yourself. But perhaps the most high-profile case of brand fanaticism in modern times was Coca-Cola's ill-fated decision to change the formula of its totemic fizzy drink on the back of positive blind tastings, only to quickly reverse the decision in the face of a massive public outcry, especially in the US, and plummeting sales.

In each of these extreme cases, the stakeholders are illustrating the link between the values of the brand and the culture in which they exist. The Macolytes invariably relate to the inferred, almost maverick creativity associated with the Mac and the fact that Apple is still portrayed as David versus Microsoft's Goliath, despite healthy performance figures. In the case of the local beer drinkers, their actions were driven less by the risk that they may not like the new beer recipe and more by a reaction to change – especially when it involved a small, local brewery, with clear, intimate associations, being subsumed into a faceless corporate. Being the plucky underdog is positive brand medicine. The Irish national brand has traded on that fact for years as, most famously, did Churchill during the darkest hours of World War II. It's also powerful brand medicine.

I've encountered similar reactions to change from customers and employees when working with brands that are closely linked to UK national brands, like British Airways, Allied Irish Bank, the Wales Tourist Board (now called Visit Wales), the Royal Navy and Royal Mail, or where the emotional ties between employees and brands are close to the surface, most obviously at charities like the children's charity the NSPCC or the animal charity, the RSPCA. One of the toughest brand refresh communication programmes I've been associated with was trying to convince reactionary RSPCA employees about the business case for making much needed basic changes to a brand they care for with a passion.

But organizations don't need an iconic product range or extreme emotional connections to achieve internal or external brand engagement on this scale.

Brand engagement is primarily about three things:

- understanding the core values that the organization stands for
- understanding the needs of customers, employees, and stakeholders that these values fulfill
- communicating a series of promises effectively, appropriately, and explicitly to both the internal and external stakeholders (and involving them in the process of determining how to fulfil those promises rather than simply turning marketing techniques inward).

Of course, sustaining that engagement is reliant upon delivery against those promises and that's an altogether different part of the journey. But who is responsible for brand engagement in the first place?

THE CEO IS DEAD, LONG LIVE THE ceo

> The top-down days are over. (David Cameron, leader of the UK Conservative Party, June 2007)

> The cult of the superhero leader is increasingly a 90s phenomenon. We've all picked up the cape these days. (line manager, ARM Holdings)

There's an old saying in England that the queen believes the world "smells of fresh paint." There's a cachet attached to the role of chief executive or CEO that exists in a similar "otherworldly" state where, superficially, there never appears to be a problem and everything is fresh, shiny, and new. It simply comes with the territory. But anyone who is familiar with the fairy tale "The Emperor's New Clothes" can appreciate that this phenomenon forewarns against a communication tragedy.

In the theatre, it's a well-known conceit that status is conferred upon an individual character, not so much by the actions of the actor

15

playing the high-status part but by the deferential actions of others. As the actor given the role of king or queen, it is your peers on stage who convey the sense of power – you can't simply project it on your own.

Businesses work in a similar way. Almost irrespective of the behavior of the person in the top job, CEO land is largely manned by a nodding, grinning, fresh-faced and wide-eyed populace and that's all down to status. As in *Hamlet*, however, methinks "something is rotten in the state."

I often relate a true story, which has sadly passed into comic legend, regarding a junior employee of a high-street retailer who, to his horror, had the misfortune of bumping into the CEO on one of his monthly "back to the floor" walkabouts. The CEO asked him, in his most empathetic tone, "so, tell me young man, who do you work for?" The starstruck employee, thinking this a trick question, could only reply "well, you, of course sir!" (much to the amusement of his colleagues, the embarrassment of the retail god, and the deep chagrin of his branch manager). It's an anecdote that gives some insight into the limitations of the hero leader's communication role.

When facilitating a top team development session geared toward breaking down the communication barriers between the board and their employees, I was greeted with the news, rather smugly relayed it must be said, of a new board initiative. In their wisdom, the board members had decided to take it in turns to compensate for their legendary lack of approachability by holding birthday lunches. In short, whenever a significant staff member's birthday fell due, they were invited to the boardroom for lunch – on the face of it, a generous and powerful gesture. I did a little checking with my consultation forum of staff and what do you think the impact had been? Soaring morale, an increase in general bonhomie? No, the absenteeism statistics for employees on and around their birthdays had increased dramatically! Who was it who first uttered the wise words, "never mistake motion for action"?

What these simple stories illustrate is that, while there isn't an explicit rule about communication between the barracks and boardroom, the specter of status never leaves the CEO's side and even when a uniquely open relationship can be maintained between the office of the CEO and more junior members of the organization, there will always be barriers to full and frank communication, based upon that powerful intangible. The rules apply in both directions but are largely created as an unspoken way of creating an "us" and an "other." Once you don the robes of senior leadership, you unwittingly become the "other," however much you may try not to. A certain brand of isolation comes with the power and the territory. The unspoken rules differ across cultures, but rules there most certainly are.

Whatever the "back to the floor" policy, if everyone the CEO meets on his weekly walkabout talks admiringly, fearing to utter a truly critical word during the dance of status, then sooner or later, loneliness and paranoia do become inevitable characteristics of new entrants to the CEO role. It takes exceptional communication skills to overcome this barrier and focusing on the CEO alone really doesn't get to the heart of the matter or address the engagement challenge.

Unfortunately, command, control, and a despotic style are often the behavioral fallback of many when faced with frustrating communication difficulties. These behavioural fallbacks certainly get people's attention, but they aren't sustainable. The great leader, however, recognizes that true engagement stems from attraction and charm, tries hard to cultivate these traits through a combination of skills development and process, but, importantly, accepts the inevitable limitations of the role – something that all the legislation in the kingdom simply can't buy. The great CEO treats his or her communication responsibilities as seriously as the other core competencies in his or her kit bag, recognizes they can't do it all on their own and instead ensures that communication is prioritized at all levels.

Accepting that very few CEOs have the capability, capacity, appetite, time, or even right to become the communication fulcrum for the business, how can anyone seriously be expected to fulfill the role of exclusive chief engagement officer, under the banner of their brand, if the internal audience never utters a critical word?

Yes, it's lonely being a CEO strutting the boards even if it's often the brand of loneliness suffered by superstars who never get no for an answer! It gives them sleepless nights. If you're in any doubt, find one and ask them. But how many CEOs have you met who truly crave the relentless spotlight and revel in its constant glare?

I believe it's time to throw away the reams written on the role of CEO as superhero communicator because:

- with a few notable exceptions, they generally aren't the best at it
- they generally can't get a straight answer by reaching down the organization
- the CEO alone really isn't the brand

- there's strong resistance to top-down communication from at least one working generation
- it's a lot more helpful to focus on the true critical mass, the line management community.

How many organizations have gambled all on the hope of a "big bang" CEO appointment, only to negotiate a severance check once the PR honeymoon is over, 18 months down the line? Whatever the hero-worshipers might say, CEOs do come and go.

Recent research by a number of consultancies and research houses has found that the average chief executive of a FTSE 100 company is in their early to mid fifties. The average age may be falling but how effective can any wealthy 50+ year old be at truly connecting with employees less than half their age and net worth? Most significantly perhaps, other research also reports that turnover of CEOs is also increasing with up to 15 percent of companies now having a change of chief executive every year. (See Lucier et al., 2002 and Egremont study, 2007).

Today's major companies are led by executives who are actually younger, show less loyalty to the company, take bigger remuneration packages, and are more dispensable than in the past. Even the legendary marathon men like BP's Lord Brown fall eventually, yet one of the marks of their greatness is that the brand lives on long after they are but a compromise agreement.

> I have always found that Angels have the vanity to speak of themselves as the only wise; this they do with a confident insolence sprouting from systematic reasoning. (William Blake, 1757–1827)

To quote an article I wrote with marketing supremo Professor Phillip Kitchen:

> Stakeholders, both internally and externally, have seen too many streetwise alley cat leaders, caught in the spotlight with the corporate cream soaking their whiskers, to rest corporate communication on just one set of shoulders.

> Irrespective of whether you're of the hero-worshipping bent or favor the more gestalt line, it's still clear that developing and sustaining corporate reputation through truly engaging communications – whether inside-out or outside-in – should be of utmost

importance to CEOs in the drive toward achieving corporate objectives. In these accountability-driven, shareholder-focused days, as the expected life-span of the species falls, they really must keep the promises they make to their stakeholders – and then make sure everyone knows about it. However it's not something they need do, or indeed should do, alone ... Far too many of today's wannabe hero-leaders remain a little too "one eyed" as they feverishly scrutinize the share price popularity polls, failing to focus on the core constituents within. If the customer really is King, isn't it worth the time and investment to ensure that the "court" is a more productive place? (Buckingham and Kitchen, 2005)

In my experience across sectors as an internal and external adviser and coach, it's the individuals who have achieved their position through establishing and maintaining functional teams, by engaging with stakeholders as with their own people, who are most able to sustain their performance levels. So why is it that so many new appointees find that no sooner do they take to the leather throne than all nonpolitical, pragmatic points of view fade? Is it any wonder that what follows is a paranoid period of soul searching to try and reconcile the avuncular, gregarious team player and friend with the character designed by the chattels of office? As the average CEO tenure continues to fall, there's very little time for them to wade through the smoke and mirrors of statistical data provided by colleagues most likely to have a vested interest in their fall.

Preparing the materials for a pan-industry engagement skills development workshop at Henley Management College, I got together with a close-knit group of experienced consultants who have worked in the people-centered consultancy industry for many years. Comparing experiences, we compiled a list of the key characteristics of senior executives we had known and worked with and who excelled at communicating. The most common traits included:

- their ability to listen and absorb
- their skill at rationalizing regular information sources into key indicators
- their love of triptych communication.

Up there at the top of the list is the willingness and ability to listen, followed by the ability to analyze information and detect patterns and then, lastly, the ability to impart information in a simple yet potent way. The last point demonstrates an ability not only to see but to point out "the wood for the trees," an innate understanding of the power of the simple yet impactful message. I once asked Patrick O'Sullivan, former CEO of Zurich in the UK, now in a senior group role, why he favored three prongs to every message when preparing his talks? He replied in typical style: "That's how I take in information myself so I'm always working with the lowest common denominator in mind."

It may be a tricky task, but many CEOs do attempt to reach down the organization for the eyes, ears, and, most importantly, the voices of the workaday custodians of the brand. Richard Branson is a famous advocate of the informal audience with the CEO and goes to great lengths to obtain employee feedback personally whenever he can, even writing to them every couple of months to encourage direct feedback, including his home contact details on the personalized letters.

But Branson is very much a one-off maverick and Virgin is exceptional for structuring its companies in small, personable units with informal but effective processes to facilitate two-way dialogue. It famously works hard on its culture, of which an informal communication style is a key component. Virgin doesn't "do its washing" in public (as one of their senior managers eloquently put it at a recent engagement event), which helps to maintain an intimate culture, and Branson credits a close executive team with helping to create an atmosphere of mutual respect and trust and preserve Branson's personal, avuncular brand. While Branson does lead by example in terms of his communication, it's clear that he expects his leaders to follow, be they in charge of an airplane or a helpline. And, in the main, they do.

It certainly helps if the chief exec is a passionate communication visionary, but he simply can't, and shouldn't, do it all himself. But internal communication is not universally respected as a discipline yet. Too often I've seen that, unless the board acknowledges that there's the same commercial rationale for focusing on communication with employees as for other strands of the corporate strategy, it's the first budget out of the basket when the "hot air balloon" hits rough weather. It always comes back to haunt them later. In the recent past, British Airways, Virgin's leading rival, despite being a market leading brand in so many areas, has found this out to its cost a number of times, as apparent internal consultation breakdowns regarding pay, security, and working conditions led to near-disastrous industrial action and have arguably adversely impacted the BA brand.

Although the industry as a whole has been under siege from external sources for some time, many of BA's recent brand problems have undoubtedly come from within. BA invest a great deal of time and effort on their internal brand and have recognized the impact these issues can potentially have on their brand and are continuously addressing any potential engagement gap.

Consider another lauded hero leader, Sir Terry Leahy, CEO of the UK's leading supermarket chain. He has transformed Tesco in the last decade to the point where profits and sales are treble what they were; the group's stock market value is around £35 billion ($70 billion) (almost nine times what it was when he took over); it has the ear of the UK government; and Tesco now competes as an international powerhouse (taking on Wal-Mart in Asia, Europe and the US); India is next. Quite a turnaround from the days when Tesco was content with capturing rival UK supermarket Sainsbury's "aspirational" customer base in the UK.

Leahy is arguably the most powerful man in his market, is certainly the most successful retailer of the last decade, and yet, far from being a heroic pin up at Tesco, he is most famous for the fact that he is still largely anonymous in his own stores. Why? Because he's much more concerned with gathering and simplifying information through listening to the people who really know, his customers and staff, than he is with self-promotion and pushing missives out to the shop floor or compliance with contrived protocol and status.

Interestingly, Leahy wrote the foreword to the visionary book *Brand Manners* (Pringle and Gordon, 2001), which carries a comprehensive case study of Tesco. In it he writes about his belief in the power of customer service and appropriate behaviors at all levels which exemplify and epitomize the ideal brand experience. He is clearly an advocate of on-brand behavior as a motivator for his customers, suppliers, stakeholders and employees alike and refers to the need for "good manners" as the cornerstone for effective relationships.

He talks about "the prospect of achieving business success by making work a better place to be." Pringle and Gordon indicate that, with 220,000 staff, Tesco's priorities back in 2001 were summed up by: mobilization and vision, "harnessing the mental energy of our people" and "having a clear, powerful and widely understood vision and values." They have come a long way.

They've certainly outperformed themselves in the last six years and it is clear that whilst processes are very important, employee engagement focused around the Tesco brand values, has been paramount. While the cynics among the analysts point to their allegedly intimidating purchasing and supplier management reputation, Leahy attributes the source of much of the success to the power of that vision of the Tesco brand, supporting behaviors and the communication surrounding it.

Leahy is famously selfless and yet his understanding of his staff and his target customer base is the stuff of business legend. He clearly owes a great deal to the controversial power of branded loyalty card data but perhaps more important is the fact that, even though he reputedly earns around £3 million ($6 million) a year, he is still comfortable being described as "the personification of his product" (empathy in action). He makes an effort not to build up brand Terry and he's as comfortable and as credible as someone in his role can be asking questions and engaging with ordinary people.

Leahy, rather like Sir Fred Goodwin at RBS, clearly prioritizes employee communication, over and above the lure of PR directed at competitors and peers. He positions himself very deliberately at the foot of the brand mountain yet is careful to role model the brand manners, values, and behaviors required of his employees. He may be famous for listening but, rather like Branson, he is role modeling a trait he expects from his employees and leaders and provides a program of development support to help deliver against this goal.

Of course, the challenges Leahy and Tesco now face are shifting in line with an awakening to the commercial realities of the environmental agenda, but, listening as ever, he is alert to the opportunities:

> You can be green and grow. Looking to the future, you may have to be green to grow. (*How Green is Your High Street*, June 2007)

But despite the pressure of corporate social responsibility being an external communication challenge, it will be fascinating to watch how Leahy engages and mobilizes his growing staff base around this new and growing ethical "mountain." Has Leahy misjudged the rapidly shifting sands of public opinion? Only time will tell, but what is clear is that however Tesco faces up to the environmental agenda, Leahy will be harnessing the power of brand-related internal communication to address the challenges they face. We watch with interest.

Whatever you may think of their organizations, their politics or personal style, there are very few executives with the ability of Leahy or Branson to reach down the organization effectively. There are few senior executives, in my experience, who haven't, instead, developed a comparatively dark art, a subtle form of inner counsel, a network of scouts who seek out the safe passages and hot spots and inadvertently help to shape strategy and policy through relaying "street" data to their leader. I'm not referring to committees, employee consultation forums and working parties that are, more often than not, a political or legislative gesture rather than a trusted partner, but to forms of personal and private counsel. This is territory that internal communication professionals should tread with caution.

Consider this quote from the CEO of a major US automotive company:

> I have my network of individuals I meet informally, individually at least once a month. This includes internal and external communications people and shop-floor cynics I can trust. The informal network includes my head of internal communication. They're normally well-rounded yet ultimately loyal folk who care enough about the time they spend at work and their relationship with me, to be honest. They're more interested in doing a worthwhile job than promotion and are themselves when they speak with me – so I trust what they say about our brand in action.

This "secret service" communication scenario is probably more common than you think. But this rather clandestine strategy also has clear limitations, not least the message it conveys about trust.

If we accept that an organization's brand is the sum of the physical and, most importantly, behavioral manifestations of the service promise it makes to its consumers, I'm afraid the sad news is that CEOs seldom trust feedback from executive peers whose jobs depend on their reports. Even at a formal level, I've seen many a new CEO tear at their hair when the incumbent FD's blanket barrage of analysis and reports are first delivered by the crate-load. Agencies and consultancies have unfortunately fallen foul of this trap, which is also why so many CEOs insist on retaining their own personal advisers and aren't really open to change. I can still picture the bearded, modestly suited, unassuming individual who was a constant presence at the elbow of the head of a global financial services company, derided and strangely feared by the board in equal measure. Yet the CEO wouldn't be without him, thought of him as his eyes and ears and, to be honest, you couldn't meet a more genuine and affable person. Oh, the tales he could tell! But did the rest of the board trust him?

Even considering the status of the figurehead, factoring in the cultural obsession with celebrity, and the extraordinary lengths some CEOs go to stay connected, the fact is that the most gifted senior communicators are, on balance, just not the most important communicators anymore.

Employees, however, are consistently and increasingly vital to reputation. They are the customer interface and, in an age of increasing systematization, all endangered touch points with fellow human beings are becoming more critical for developing and sustaining brand. When the customer has a need and/or succumbs to the advertising, responds to the brand's projected values, and comes face to face with an automated process, process engineers and frontline employees are absolutely vital. This means that the leaders who communicate with them the most frequently, either directly or through their teams, are the key communicators in any business. Increasingly, this is the line management community. But, arguably, frontline communication standards have slipped – a big brand issue.

When the smoke has cleared from the latest brand launch and the troupe of performing artists has packed up its Queen CDs and moved on, when the last sound bite from the trend-setting webcast has lost its teeth, when the last "customer first" mug has finally cracked in the corporate dishwasher, employees alone will remain the keepers or breakers of the promises that organizations make to customers, whatever the CEO says. In an age of mission statements, high-profile, often high-tech guerilla communication and supposedly visionary leadership, the chief engagement officer role has expanded dramatically. Now, more than ever, all line managers are chief engagement officers in their interactions with staff and all employees become chief engagement officers in every customer interaction.

Internal communication specialist, Melcrum, who have a global network of around 20,000 internal communication stakeholders, undertook an Employee Engagement study in 2005 and asked respondents to choose the top three most important drivers of engagement. Interestingly, the top result was still senior leadership (what I'm calling hero leaders), but was closely followed by direct supervisors or line managers. This is the first time they have asked the question so they don't have comparative data, but it won't be long before their rankings are reversed

What this does illustrate is that face-to-face communication from credible sources is absolutely key, with formal internal communication (which is largely tactical) coming well down the list. A tricky conundrum for many communicators who still have their sights locked on the tactical level.

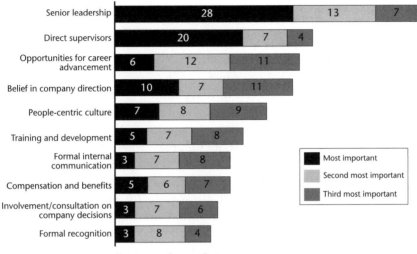

Percentage of respondents

FIGURE 1.1 **Top 10 drivers of employee engagement (all data from companies that conduct a key driver analysis)**

Source: Employee Engagement © Melcrum Publishing, 2005

With the need for more adaptive behavior to meet changing customer demands, employees, rather than board members, have become the vital ingredient in how missions are accomplished.

Bennis (1997, taken from Buckingham and Kitchen, 2005) states:

> What effective leaders are going to have to do is to create not just a vision, but a vision with meaning ... The vision has to be shared. And the only way that it can be shared is for it to have meaning for the people who are involved in it.

The key point is in the last sentence – for a vision to be shared, it needs "to have meaning for the people who are involved in it." It's relatively easy when you've written the battle plan to watch the action unfold on a distant plain and just as easy to criticize the decisions of the generals if you're not party to the factors behind the orders. It's often overlooked that the process of working together across hierarchies in the very act of involvement is probably the key driver of engagement and that it's frankly not something that you can cascade. Engagement simply has to be built from the ground up and it means getting very involved in the action.

ARE WE AT THE TAIL END OF SPIN?

We live in an era of political, military and socioeconomic spin (the act of providing an interpretation of a statement or event, in a way that subtly conveys bias so as to sway opinion). We may be approaching the tail end of that era as there's a great deal of evidence to show that this veneer is wearing extremely thin. Just as customers are becoming increasingly intolerant of spin, employees (who, of course, are consumers themselves) have little time for employer branding focused on aligning them with scripted messages, descending like favors from above.

This last point was graphically illustrated recently when I was asked to review and report back on the impact of a vision communication cascade. The request was from the central communications function of a global engineering company. When the expensive, slickly designed video of the chairman, CEO and board, filmed talking from a carefully designed script at a range of international locations (you know the sort of thing I'm referring to), was played to the subsidiaries in Eastern Europe, it was met with an angry silence. This was soon followed by cold hostility in the feedback forum. What had been perceived as a benevolent act of engagement by the central team was compared to politburo tactics by the Eastern line managers. They had failed, as a result, to pick up any of the many positive messages in the piece.

Furthermore, employees the world over are extremely intolerant of overdesigned initiatives that cost more than the severance packages of their colleagues. If employees are to engage with and support the vision and claims made by corporate and brand communications, they need to be treated with respect. Communication must be authentic and tailored to local markets, and recognition must be given to the fact that line managers are the workaday communication "superheroes." Line managers and supervisors, the noncommissioned officers of the corporate machine, have to make sense of the world for their people if they're to help the strategy work. They can't do that with spin and internal PR, largely because they have to look their team members in the eyes every day. Pity the poor divisional director of a professional services firm who recently had to run an expensively designed team briefing session about employment brand when her department, the operations function, was officially called "Burden" on the structure chart.

If brand engagement is to be truly achieved, local ceos, irrespective of level, need to know how they fit in. They need to understand their importance to the corporation, and willingly translate this into supportive attitudes, behavior, and positive word of mouth. Communication needs to be recognized, measured, and rewarded as a core competency. Clearly, clumsy attempts to align and control will eventually prove unsustainable and ultimately breed creeping brand death through cultural stagnation, corruption, failure to innovate, and even sabotage. If you doubt it, remember Barings, BCCI, the Shell reserves crisis, the Firestone tires debacle, Enron, the recent television telephone competition scandals – even dare to remember Abu Ghraib.

WHAT CHARACTERIZES AN EFFECTIVE CHIEF ENGAGEMENT OFFICER?

According to Fombrun (1996), the top traits of companies that employees would like to work for are:

- they promote trust
- they empower employees
- they inspire pride.

But what are employees saying now?

In 2005, my consultancy, the Bring Yourself 2 Work Fellowship (BY2W) surveyed 1,500 employees in CEO roles (defined as anyone with pivotal communications responsibility from board members through to line managers). When we asked respondents to reflect on corporate communication and relay best practices, we discovered that the traits they most admire in leaders who they consider to be effective at engaging with employees include (in ranking order):

- openness
- bravery

- honesty
- charisma.

Conversely, the characteristics that they see as hindering effective engagement from both a personal and corporate perspective are prioritized as:

- one-way communication and lack of involvement
- insincerity and spin
- inaction
- failure to personalize messages to key audiences (blanket bombing).

In leadership terms, social development has long been determining a shift away from the era of authoritarian leadership – defined by obedience to authority at the expense of personal liberty. We are now in the age of authentic leadership, driven by a need to believe and to trust. The communication role of the chief executive, in communication terms, is more *primus inter pares* than presidential now. How fast the transition happens and how effective it will be will rest significantly on the degree to which leaders can engage their employees by connecting with their emotional as well as rational selves.

Authoritarian organizations arguably still have their place, but it's increasingly questionable whether they're getting the best out of their people, and when authoritarian cultures appear on the corporate radar, it's more often than not a signal that something's awry! Even the armed forces are having to adapt their leadership style to bring out the best in their recruits.

Bill George (2003), in *True North*, one of the seminal texts on this subject, defines the concept of authentic leadership as, in effect, being true to yourself. This means understanding and being true to your values, finding your own style, and ensuring that there is appropriate fit between your values and the organization you represent. He refers to five dimensions:

1. Understanding and pursuing your purpose with passion
2. Practicing solid values
3. Leading with your heart
4. Establishing connected relationships
5. Demonstrating self-discipline.

Being your own person is absolutely key, it allows the leader to be objective and independent. Understanding what the real you is can be an altogether trickier undertaking. Clarifying the true culture and values of your organization is a great deal more complex than consulting the marketing literature; but ensuring that the real you fits with the brand of your organization is the trickiest proposition of all. Authentic leadership is the central challenge facing anyone in a leadership role, who is concerned with brand management and believes that employee engagement is the key to effective brand management. It is the challenge that now faces true ceos, or as Caroline Hempstead, AstraZeneca's VP, group corporate communication, and what I call a true Tier 1 communication professional puts it:

The best role models and most effective communicators I've known are all:

- astute business leaders who are positive about engagement, not just pushing information
- good at simplifying and staying on message, linking information to develop a consistent story, adapted for audiences
- comfortable in their own skin, so their communication is authentic and consistent with other aspects of their leadership style
- as good at listening as they are communicating
- being themselves and, therefore, they're inspirational but also predictable which adds to the credibility of the message.

The acid test always is "would I follow this person into battle?" That's a characteristic which owes a lot to integrity and authenticity rather than being a slick communicator.

SUMMARY OF KEY LEARNINGS

- Brands are more about people than process and their management has global implications
- Line managers are the new hero communicators
- Authentic communication that delivers at both the emotional and rational levels is the most powerful and most engaging communication

5 Things to Try Today

1. Be clear about the organization's purpose and values.
2. Ask yourself how your own values square with 1.
3. Find a way to understand where your staff (and customers) are at.
4. Seek out and promote great brand engagement role models (don't be blinded by seniority).
5. Imagine yourself giving a rallying speech and then charging headlong into battle, flags and bullets flying. You take a look around you. Who's still there?

Tim Bulmer (2007) *Brand Alignment Workshop*

ACT 2

DECONSTRUCTING BRAND ("BUT WE DON'T EVEN BRAND ANIMALS ANY MORE")

Everyman is watching business breakfast TV out of the corner of his eye. Someone has just sold an obscure Lowry painting for over a million dollars and he finds himself humming that awful song "Matchstick men and matchstick cats and dogs." Funny how the most annoying tunes get filed away in the memory. The images are very familiar – the long lines of people bent double, trudging to the mills in northern England. "What's the attraction of having something like that on your wall, depressing, naive art? A million dollars eh!?" he mutters into the mirror while he finishes his tie.

Everyman's eye darts instinctively to the clock on the TV. "Damn, I'm late" (it's 7 a.m.).

Throwing his toast and just-sipped coffee in the sink, with one well-rehearsed movement he slips his grey jacket over one white-shirted arm and opens the front door, stopping to hurriedly scrunch on his black work brogues at the threshold.

Leaving his exclusive, former docker's brownstone cottage safely tucked into the gated development of one-bedroom apartments, he thinks of his wife who will be well on the road to her first appointment by now. "Looks like the congestion is as bad as yesterday," he thinks to himself, not noticing that he's now part of a steady flow of smart suits streaming to the subway.

He has grown accustomed to the rhythms of the journey. The solace in the crowd, the time with his own thoughts and work reports in the tunnel and then the adrenalin rush at the other end as the high-rise office blocks draw him through their doors with their intimidating, brash energy.

In the packed lift up to his floor, he reflects on the hive of activity promised by today's diary – rotating team briefing cascade, the O&M consultants and process management drive, the five meetings in one-hour slots, the new brand video show in the conference room, the performance appraisals, and, always somewhere, the constant pulse of punctuating phone calls. To cap it all, he's been asked to input to a values and culture development review process. "HR nonsense, don't they have any work to do? Might see what I can do to get out of that one."

As he is sucked from the lift by the slipstream of his colleagues, he reflects for a second on his title "manager." What an odd word to pin on someone who can barely manage his own complicated space, and just then two of his team rise from their seats with questions brimming. As he moves, nods, and listens, he can't get that damn "Matchstick men" song out of his head.

BRAND AND AUTHENTICITY

Having established the power shift in responsibility for communication in Act 1, Act 2 explores the triumvirate relationship between communication, motivation, and brand.

What is an organization but a collection of people who have been brought together to achieve a goal? The goal is communicated to customers, via external communication disciplines like marketing, and to staff, if they're lucky, via internal communication.

What is a brand but a range of perceptions in the mind of the consumer, whether they're a customer or a member of staff? Despite the reams of complicated analysis in the market, it's essentially simple, even primal stuff.

This view of brand is summed up, for me, by what I call the "authenticity equation." This is, quite simply, the relationship between the promises made as they relate to the goals of the business, minus the performance delivered against that promise.

The authenticity equation
BRAND PROMISE minus SERVICE = BRAND AUTHENTICITY
EMPLOYER BRAND minus EMPLOYEE BRAND = EMPLOYMENT BRAND AUTHENTICITY

The equation of promise made versus experience delivered applies equally to both the internal and external stakeholder markets, whether the organization is selling goods and services or selling an employment brand ("what it's really like to work here"). A true brand is a promise post delivery, not what we aspire it to be.

Once upon a time owners ran businesses, managers ran staff, and staff ran as slowly as they could get away with in order to earn an honest wage and then they went home and put the whole experience out of their minds. There was a certainty and structure about the relationships, as they largely mirrored the prevailing social order. A lot has changed in a relatively short time.

The complexity of business management seems to multiply with each passing decade and, while it's certainly tough at the top, I would argue that the business of leading within organizations increases in complexity the further the leader is drawn away from the core purpose, the goal. As such, the importance of communication should rise exponentially as responsibility for leadership ripples outward from the core. This places a great deal of responsibility on the shoulders of line managers and customer contact staff who, perversely, are often the least empowered, recognized or well rewarded. That, as they say, is the "elephant in the room" of many of today's businesses, a great big lumbering bull elephant dressed in customer service clothing.

The evolution of society has brought about different models for leading, based upon the patterns of interactions and the links between technology, tasks and people. Organizational structure specialists like Gareth Morgan lead us to believe that what we have come to call "command and control" models largely evolved from military or imperialist approaches to organizational structure. Theories relating to organization models generally reflect a range from the rigid, top-down functional bureaucracy (the stuff of empire), through the matrix organization and usually culminate in the loosely coupled organic (the behavioral network of hub and spokes). These extremes are illustrated in Figure 2.1.

The way in which the structure of internal communication functions has evolved over the past decade or so loosely follows this pattern. The structure has slowly changed as the nature of the role has changed, with the vast majority now moving toward the network model as competence, confidence and impact have all improved.

This has partly been in response to the evolution of the organizational infrastructure that drives internal communication – tracking the movement from the mouthpiece for the king of the bureaucracy through to the self-managing, devolved hive of the organic network where stories now emerge from the heart of the culture at all levels.

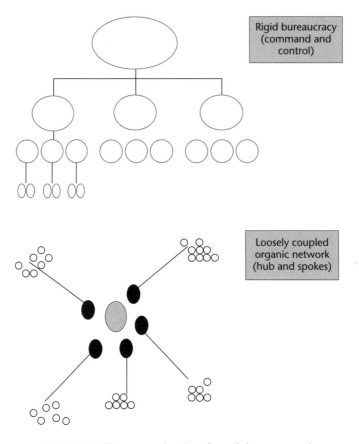

FIGURE 2.1 **Two organizational models compared**

But despite changes to the communication architecture, the relationship between brand and people, from an individual through to team level and onward, has been a constant, long before organizations evolved to manage them (Figure 2.2).

This simple diagram, based upon a combination of research and consultancy practice, represents an approximation of the head space each of us roughly affords brand-related thought. It includes key decisions we make regarding our purchases, linked to a combination of our hopes, desires, thoughts, aspirations, beliefs, and values.

We may all change the order somewhat depending on our life stage and situation (times of national crisis, for example, or whether we have dependants), but most people have been able to relate roughly to the order and weighting.

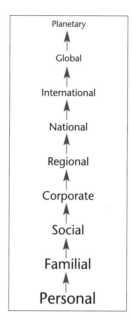

FIGURE 2.2 **The macro-brand hierarchy**

Existentialism and free-market economics attempt to convince us that we're self-determining, which would suggest that, as individuals, we should be conscious of and responsible for the image we project, values we adopt, and decisions we make, including the brands we buy into. Sometimes as consumers or employees we're happy to abdicate responsibility for our brand decisions, conveniently forgetting our existential responsibilities, and occasionally blame the marketers of products, services and ultimately jobs for decisions we make.

Part of the clue to authentic brand engagement is to confront this willing abdication of responsibility and rediscover differentiating criti-cal faculties as a route to empowerment and self-determinism in ourselves and our people which are both drivers of performance and self-esteem. Although this isn't always as easy as it sounds. But given the scale of the need to change, which has now moved well beyond the corporate level in the brand hierarchy, we're shortly going to have little other choice.

Interestingly, however, most discussion about brand centers on corporate brand – largely because that's where most of the money is and where our current obsessions lie. I believe it's also because the corporate brand usually represents a depersonalized "other," a comfortable, almost neutral territory about which it's safe to talk without really engaging. This is sadly where a great deal of corporate brand engagement training, particularly training which has crossed national boundaries, is focused at the expense of true engagement, and this depersonalized neutral territory is where most delegates are content to hide. This is the primary reason for the ultimate failure of internal brand engagement programs, costing millions. We need to remember the golden thread that runs back into the deep forest of social evolution if we're to truly understand our relationship with brands and how we can influence the ways we engage with them.

BRAND ANTHROPOLOGY

It is a primal instinct to leave our mark on things. We want to "leave a legacy," make a name, be remembered, make something our own – to brand something as our own. It's a deeper desire than simply owning someone else's brand as a way of making a statement, but comes from the same stable of wants. Self-branding is a deeply revealing act, whether through the way we influence our offspring and loved ones: through imprinting ourselves on the short-term memories of others as part of our banal modern obsession with fame, or through fashion (with, for example, something as dramatic as a tattoo – a practice that has witnessed a considerable surge in popularity in the past decade), or friendships, clubs, speech or lifestyle choices. It's often easier to follow the lead of others.

The rise of ethnography and anthropology in business is testimony to the fact that communication behaviors have deep-seated roots and that core principles change surprisingly little. As recently as February 2007, a paper titled "Anthropology as Brand" was presented at Oxford University. And there's a growing bibliography in this field. Anthropology getting in on the act may be quite ironic but not all that surprising. Research any society or period, however sophisticated it may appear to be, and the pattern persists of individuals differentiating themselves within groups and yet preserving common traditions and mores that ensure their fit within the prevailing culture. This combination of behavioral and physical discrimination, assimilation and differentiation is nothing if it isn't brand. Brand development certainly isn't a 20th-century invention.

Mankind has instinctively sought to differentiate itself from "others." It's one of the earliest representations of self-determinism, be it through distinctive signs, ciphers, flags or, perhaps more powerfully, behavioral traits that become norms, help the group to bond, and simultaneously identify one group from the next.

Many social signals translate well within the species, even across cultures. The best brands obey the same rules, when design and values, process and behaviors work in harmony to send out the right signals. If the prevailing Zeitgeist is one of conspicuous consumption, we can hardly blame brand managers for waving the flag of bacchanalian avarice. But brand managers and internal chief engagement officers need to keep their fingers on the stakeholder pulse or run the risk of waving a flag on a deserted battlefield. Anyone designing brand engagement workshops should take particular note and ensure that they create space for a meaningful exploration of the link between personal brand and the corporate equivalent if they're looking to do more than raise awareness.

We are entering a very rare age indeed, when corporate branding may well be outflanked and usurped by issues of national, international and even global import. The brand hierarchy is feeling the strain.

As recently as June 2007, some of Europe's largest firms, including banks HBOS and ABN Amro, oil company BP and consultancy firms Ernst & Young and Deloitte, met in London to talk about how to motivate their employees to adopt green practices. The seminar, entitled Going Green: Inspiring People, included Anthony Day, environmental champion and author, who was quoted as saying that "internal communications are key to making companies more eco-friendly" and talked about the power of education and corporations leading by example by engaging with employees (according to the website www.livingethically.co.uk).

As far back as 2004, in its *Organic Food and Farming Report*, the UK's Soil Association reported that retail sales of organic food were growing at twice the rate of nonorganic, increasing by £2 million per week, and total sales were £1.12 billion (close to $2 billion). But, according to the UK's Organic Farmers & Growers, in its *National Benchmark Survey of Organic Food Production* published in August 2004, from a sample of 1,144 registered organic farmers who responded to the survey, the following was reported:

- 4 percent described their business profitability as healthy
- 21 percent described it as moderate
- 33 percent described it as low

- 30 percent described it as borderline
- 12 percent described it as unviable.

It doesn't take a sage to see that there's a clear values and ethics-based coincidence of wants here for the retail and agriculture sectors clearly, and for any brand manager looking to connect with employees through appealing to changing personal values. I've seen the impact of this particular phenomenon on brands I've worked with recently like the UK's Energy Saving Trust, which had considerably greater success in engaging both internal and external audiences with its recent "Save your 20 per cent" advertising campaign, informed by employee and customer consultation, than they may have previously expected. There has also been a significant rise in the popularity of farmers' markets, a phenomenal resurgence of the "grow your own" mentality, interestingly the most significant reawakening in self-sufficiency since the last world war, and a proliferation of food hero awards, with celebrity chefs like Jamie Oliver and Rick Stein rousing middle England, in particular, to seek out producers of ethically produced, wholesome, organic produce.

This values-based phenomenon is finally opening routes to competitive advantage for organizations like the ethical retailer Abel & Cole (UK Organic Retailer of the Year 2004). Its superb customer-first mentality, empowering, bespoke service and door-to-door deliveries of ethically farmed, realistically priced, and environmentally friendly produce is now in tune with the values and lifestyles of an important consumer market, who would sooner fund smaller producers than increasingly infamous corporate retail brands. It's no coincidence that Abel & Cole's innovative, back-to-basics customer service is fast becoming the stuff of customer service lore.

The impact of values-based purchasing is being felt in a number of sectors and by a host of brands. In particular, climate change and corporate social responsibility are significant issues for consumers, and many are willing to change their investment habits as a result, according to research by Norwich Union. A study, conducted on behalf of Norwich Union by Ipsos MORI (Michaelis, 2007), revealed that more than half the people surveyed (57 percent) are interested in long-term financial products, such as savings, ISAs and pensions, where the fund managers choose investments that take account of the impact on climate change. Eleven percent said they would be interested in ethical investment, regardless of the effect it might have on their financial return. The research also showed that two-thirds

(66 percent) of people think insurance companies and pensions providers should offer products to limit the effect of climate change, and two-thirds (67 percent) said these companies should provide their customers with information on what they can do to limit the effects of climate change.

Dr Peter Michaelis, manager of the Norwich Union UK Ethical fund and Norwich Union Sustainable Future UK Growth funds, said (Michaelis, 2007):

> Climate change is a hugely important issue and barely a day goes by without a leading politician or news story highlighting the scale of the problem. This research shows how important an issue it is for consumers and how people are now willing to make changes to reduce its impact.

Dr Michaelis continued:

> People who are concerned about climate change should be aware that their investment decisions can play a significant role in reducing their own carbon footprint.

For "hugely important," we can also read "potentially profitable" so long as the margins are invested in a way that reinforces the values that informed the purchase.

Clearly, tapping into humanistic brand attributes and communicating values in tune with the times is an age-old marketing ploy. Why then can't this power be harnessed to further both commercial and humanistic ends? Increasingly apocalyptic scientific evidence suggests that only by leveraging our skills at helping to shape consumer choice, but for the greater rather than just individual good, may we start to redress the ethical imbalance within and across nations, as well as (and let's not forget this) drive complementary competitive differentiation.

Tree hugging may have had a bad press in the past but, ironically, it's big brand business right now and for the foreseeable future. The point, however, is that there's a strong business case for clarifying and positioning values and ethics at the forefront of brand communication within both the internal and external markets, not as a concession to the HR lobby but as an increasingly important route to authentic engagement. Employee engagement is virtually impossible without this emotional dimension; it simply becomes "tick box" communication focused more on volume than achievement of objectives.

FIGURE 2.3 **Brand anthropology**

NEW WAYS OF TELLING OLD STORIES

Cinema has been particularly successful in plugging into the mythology underpinning this sentient, values-based desire to be engaged. Epic genre movies, like *Braveheart, The Matrix* series, *Harry Potter* or the *Star Wars* saga, all exploit the rebel mentality – plucky pioneer versus empire – through lavish use of the maverick metaphor, the irreverent underdog against the oppressive, controlling "other." They all leverage our innate desire to belong, our primal understanding of the rules of engagement, the rules of storytelling, and the indomitable power of mythology. We don't always admit it but we all inadvertently bring the same rules to corporate communication. Leaders clearly need to be cognizant of the fact that brand thinking has its roots in our most primary social engagements – we do it instinctively.

One of the classic cinematic representations of this phenomenon in action is the genesis scene in the 1968 science fiction film directed by Stanley Kubrick, *2001: A Space Odyssey*, where the action starts in 4 million BC and morphs from tribal apes, who, characterized by fear, curiosity, and courage, discover a savage new use for basic tools, to the sexy icons of earthmen in space where society comes under direct attack from the supercomputer HAL 9000.

Kubrick's film is a less than subtle allegory, critiquing our obsession with materialism at the expense of higher order values, and, although it was made in the 1960s, remains hugely relevant today. The movie is both a warning and a signpost to a more palatable alternative, although, rather pessimistically, it does convey a sense that we're essentially doomed to repeat our mistakes.

Storytelling and mythology are tools that leaders need to employ with due care and attention. As the master storyteller Joseph Campbell (2001) explains: "mythology is the sum of the stories people tell to make sense of the universe and our place in it." That's a pretty powerful reason to listen; making storytelling a potent way of capturing our attention as it engages with the natural laws of communication and taps into our primal forces of motivation.

It's pretty important that we understand how the rules and rhythms operate, if we're to retain our critical faculties as consumers and maximize our communication as professionals, as ceos, and brand managers.

LEADERSHIP ENGAGEMENT

The communal compulsion to make sense of the corporate universe lies at the heart of values-based coaching models, for example, which look to develop and reinforce "on-brand" leadership behavior. Leaders need to be the visible architects of any drive toward trend-setting behavior change. They need to be the collective owners of the culture, so it stands to reason that they stand at the head of the engagement queue.

Being able to tap into the power of assimilation and differentiation simultaneously is one of the arts behind successful employee engagement. But it's an art that should always start with the true engagement of the leadership team before even considering mass rollout of "totemic" engagement events.

Leadership team development activities in support of true brand engagement need to address each of the following five stations as part of a behavioral "contract":

1. Primary purpose (why we are here)
2. Leadership processes (how we operate)
3. Foundations of leadership (how we lead)
4. Leadership team (how we interact)
5. Individual behavior (how I behave).

Coaching support must recognize that the leadership team members simultaneously inhabit two realities:

- the outer world of corporate rationalism and
- the inner or personal world which is likely to be a lot closer to the emotional core.

An effective, values-based coaching process will explore both realities and help to delicately bridge the gap between corporate and personal values in pursuit of superior performance. This is undoubtedly the most effective route to an effective and lasting leadership performance culture.

In exploring each of the five stations – contracting and bonding with each other, structuring expectations, understanding stakeholder needs and abilities, experimenting with new ways of interacting, agreeing plans and developing the story of the leadership team and their hopes and ambitions for the business – the group has to understand that they are reenacting a process that has been played out many times before.

They aren't alone. But to fail to take a coordinated approach to team development that balances processes and behaviors will have inevitable dysgenic effects. This is a common issue, most explicitly seen within family businesses, which quite frequently fail to manage the emotional issues underpinning their brand especially regarding succession and the transfer of power because the issues are so much closer to the surface and literally closer to home.

Development activity at each station needs to work off the last link in the chain and reinforce the next. The development process has to be seen as a holistic exercise, constantly referencing the overall purpose, goals, culture and values, and needs to take into account the impact on the representation of the brand, first internally and then externally. Too many activities of this nature never make it past the rational, process-driven stages or, at the other end of the scale, delve too deeply into the emotional too quickly or without appropriate support or structure. This absence of a holistic approach is partly why so much engagement related management development activity has such a poor reputation.

There are positioning risks when playing with primal branding impulses, not least as the natural rhythms and innate learned structures demand that the story defines an "us" (the community on behalf of whom the central character is questing) and an "other" (the archetypes who bring threat, risk, fear, and challenge). Fail to understand the attitude and appetite of the audience or don't clearly identify the true root cause of dissatisfaction and the "other" can very quickly become the leadership team (or from the perspective of the leadership team, the staff or even customers, without whom it would "be so much simpler to run this business," as I heard a senior manager say recently).

The story has to be carefully developed and positioned if the energy of the community is to be directed to best effect. Engagement is something you shortcut at your peril. The current private equity debate, for example, will be an interesting case to follow, especially when the leadership teams who continue to receive record bonus payments are called upon to dip into the pool of employee or customer goodwill at the next mass engagement event. Who will be the "us" and who the "other," I wonder?

This compulsion to assimilate and differentiate simultaneously is no more powerfully illustrated than in a very simple role-playing exercise for groups.

The MANAGER game

A group of up to 20 people of roughly the same status are split into two groups, taken to different rooms, and then given a briefing sheet. The text is identical and includes a simple problem-solving exercise (an office reorganization, preparation for a VIP visit, designing a logo and so on). The only difference is in the title on the forms:

- Group A – briefing for managers
- Group B – briefing for staff.

The groups are left on their own to react to the exercise.

It's remarkable how patterns of behavior repeat themselves, irrespective of organization, sector or experience of the participants. Invariably the "staff" group members, robbed of context (the story), fall into caricatures and quickly adopt abdication and subservient persona, use the time to rebel against the exercise, joke and play games until they eventually become bored, make up their own context and self-select to work on the exercise themselves and/or hunt down the managers.

The managers, on the other hand, almost always lock the door, wear the responsibility heavily and seriously, spend time arguing over roles and agreeing a story between them as an alibi for their actions, give themselves targets and time limits and always set out to solve the problem before they consider what the other group is doing. They usually believe that they are in competition somehow and that it's their job to have all the answers. When they're told that the other group is "the staff," the managerial group invariably meets any approach by the other group with officiousness, insisting that they aren't interrupted, and, if they are to meet at all, make a point of dictating time, venue, room layout, and agenda.

It takes very little prompting for people to behave in line with what they perceive to be the behavioral brand of the role, to create a group identity based on archetypes and largely defined in counterpoint to "the other."

Terry Gilliam's haunting black comedy-cum-satire *Brazil* is one of the most memorable representations of this phenomenon in practice and, like all great art, wouldn't have the same impact if it didn't have more than a grain of truth in it. Remember the scene when the Everyman anti-hero Sam Lowry finally finds his grey, characterless new office on the first day of his new job? He is soon involved in a tug of war trying to prevent his desk disappearing into the wall, the other side of which is a fellow junior executive, threatened by the new appointee and attempting desperately to assert his own status by anonymously tugging as much of the shared desk through to his own side of the partitioned office as he can.

Gilliam may have exotic tastes and has been criticized as someone prone to melodramatize the human condition, but I've certainly witnessed the sentiments (if not the exact actions) behind this scene played out countless times. The most recent performance was at a German engineering firm where I was visiting their leadership team to help them develop a communication approach for their new diversity policy, one of the elements of a strategy to widen the appeal of their brand. I met their recently appointed, only female executive who boasted that she had just celebrated her groundbreaking elevation to the all-male board by having the partition in her new office expanded to give her four windows; one more than any of her male colleagues, as befitting her status. She then proceeded to speak without a hint of irony about the company's diversity policy, approach to employee recognition, and the need to overcome the pitfalls of the past and tap into the emotional equity in its brand values.

Although I'm a great advocate of working with the prevailing culture as a means of subsequently influencing change from within, examples like this, rather like squabbling over managerial car parking or executive chairs, can lead to little other than a pyrrhic victory in the interface between status and culture. Don't become obsessed with them but do treat organizational totems with great care.

As we've developed as individuals and as social beings, our identification mechanisms have evolved to the point that in our modern society, consumer brands exploit our innate social associations and aspirational mentality, feeding on our instinctive ability to draw on social archetypes as points of reference ("a manager like me, who stands for these values, drives this brand of car" and so on). In the modern world, brands have largely dominated the pinnacle of the differentiation "food chain." The consumer brand frenzy has certainly become all the more frenetic in the past two decades.

As chief engagement officers, we all need to be aware that:

- brand awareness is an innate skill; differentiation and assimilation are basic desires

- the formula for engagement is natural; we all instinctively understand and employ the rules daily
- individuals are the pivot for brands and have the power to make or break them.

BRANDS AND MOTIVATION

In *The Hungry Spirit*, Charles Handy (1997) calls upon the work of Francis Kinsman to help put the materialistic 1980s in some form of sociological context.

Kinsman used three psychological types developed by the Stanford Research Institute to describe personal motivation:

1. *Sustenance driven* – where the prime objective is financial and social security.
2. *Outer directed* – high achievers driven by esteem and status, drawn to materialistic symbols of their perceived success.
3. *Inner directed* – motivated by expression of their innate talents and beliefs and concerned with ethics and how society is run.

Kinsman used this research to explain the gradual shift throughout the 1990s, onward and upward from avaricious consumerism toward more spiritual self-fulfillment and self-expression, a steady movement that has undoubtedly gained fresh impetus recently in the face of global imperatives like the technology explosion, the environmental agenda, and conflict over faith and ideologies.

I'll illustrate this point further by referencing one of the pivotal and most impactful psychological theories to have emerged in modern times.

Maslow's hierarchy of needs emerged as a psychological theory in the 1940s yet it's seldom left the organization development spotlight since as a means of understanding human motivation. It is normally depicted as a five-leveled pyramid with the pinnacle being growth needs, the realm of self-actualization (morality, creativity and so on). The other four levels are what he terms deficiency needs, largely physiological necessities which are the basic requirements for existence. These deficiency needs range from eating, drinking and procreating through to security, belonging and relationships and the development of confidence, esteem and respect.

The basic premise is that people evolve over time from being obsessed with satisfying needs at the base of the pyramid through to the gradual progression toward fulfillment of higher order needs, the pinnacle of our evolution. However, should the lower order needs come under significant threat (as in a redundancy or badly managed change scenario), people theoretically drop down the hierarchy to address that need again. It's an instinctive defensive action which all change managers need to understand.

Using Maslow's hierarchy as a reference point, I believe that we can begin to expose the limitations of silo brand thinking, which is either obsessed with the physical and the rational and the customer perspective or fails to recognize the spiritual, behavioral, and employee perspective. Only by appreciating the need for a holistic approach to brand management will we be able to start to visualize the true route to engagement.

The status-obsessed, process-led approach to brand management seeks to construct a vision at the top and gradually cascade compliance throughout the organization. It's an approach that seeks to establish alignment and weed out nonconformance, largely playing on the power of hierarchical instruction and fear of difference to achieve compliance. I refer to this phenomenon as the engagement filter, reflecting the fact that it only truly fulfils the higher order needs of the senior leaders and fails to engage junior employees as a result (see Figure 2.4).

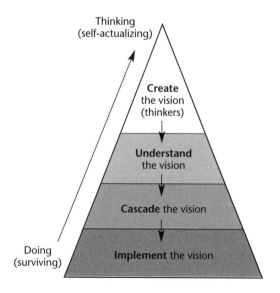

FIGURE 2.4 **The engagement filter**

49

Mapped to Maslow's hierarchy, the approach effectively says: "We're at the top of the pyramid and have the luxury of contemplating and addressing the big, important issues. This is our vision. We're passing on our wisdom to the senior managers because they're important enough and will include their trusted team members. Everyone has a part to play but if you don't conform and align to our vision, there will be consequences." It's an approach suited to the command and control management model and it's an approach trapped in time. It fails on so many different levels, the most significant being that the privileged authors of the vision are necessarily and literally "in a different place" from the lowly employees expected to implement it.

It's interesting to note that leaders like Tesco's Terry Leahy understand the visual power of the metaphor and describe themselves as being effectively at the foot of the pyramid or at the bottom of the mountain looking up rather than perched at the pinnacle. But so many organizations still persist with this push approach to brand engagement. Whether it's down to vain efforts to avoid inefficiencies, fear of facing up to difficult questions or concern at the effort required to understand and develop truly engaging communication, mystifies me. Combine this compulsion with the undisputed fact that a hierarchical push system is woefully inefficient in driving authentic engagement and long-term change and is it any surprise that so many legends persist of infamous rebrand launches or vision programs staggering beneath the weight of their own administration or overbalancing as a result of a top-heavy emphasis?

Sculpting sound bites within newsrooms and authorship by committee may well spread the weight of responsibility but also ensure that passionate imperatives are replaced with cold logic as rational, sanitized forms of words are "normalized." This would go some way to explain the glaring lack of originality in cascaded vision statements and passionless values declarations.

Internal communication in cascade cultures, even when undertaken as well as it can be, does convey a sense of "what's in it for you?" But a dry relay of facts does little more than appeal to the "baser needs" like security, the package, and, if you're lucky, pride and trust. Ironically, this type of communication, if handled badly (like the outputs of a benefits review cascaded programmatically without an engaging context), usually signals that the baser needs will probably come under threat shortly as part of a drive for "change."

Using Kinsman's terminology, the business imperative is expressed in a way to appeal to the sustenance needs (basic job security, protection of pay and benefits), and the aspirational goal appeals at best to the outer-directed consciousness of employees (outperforming competitors, being the best within the company and so on). There's little to appeal to the higher order growth needs illustrated in Maslow's hierarchy and which increasingly sophisticated employees crave. Podium-bashing "fight or flight" communication can only engender relatively short bursts of energy (handy if you're a chief executive with a short-term goal). But the key to mobilizing the business in pursuit of long-term goals is to appeal to inner-directed, higher order needs and this takes care, attention, time, and, most importantly, the top team to be engaged and committed advocates themselves.

But all too often, these higher order needs are derided as:

- expensive luxuries
- weaknesses
- effeminate
- complicated to manage
- something you do at home, not at work.

What's more expensive and complicated to manage than a failed mass brand engagement event which spends a fortune delivering a single golden bullet but fails to connect with employees and doesn't have a lasting positive impact on the brand? Isn't it worth taking the time to do the groundwork properly before launching into the creative implementation? We may think we've made significant strides as a society, but when you look beyond the internal PR and spin or the brand labels on our purchases, how far have we really shuffled up Maslow's hierarchy? The challenges for the communication community are manifold.

If you consider that, certainly in the UK (and this applies in other countries), three generations are working together (baby boomers born 1942–65, Generation X born 1966–79, and Generation Y, the millennials), it's simply no longer possible to take a blanket approach to employee engagement based on cascades from the top. The internal stakeholder motivators are so diverse that the strutting, presidential CEO is as likely to be "bottled off the stage" as applauded.

Jonathan Austin, chief executive of Best Companies, which compiles the *Sunday Times 100 Best Companies to Work For* supplement, is quoted in *The Times*, May 2007, as saying:

Gen Y people are looking for organizations that offer more than money ... our data shows they are looking for a working environment in which they can continue to learn. They also want flexibility and a real work–life balance. They simply aren't looking to mortgage their lives to the company.

I would argue that this really isn't much different to what other employees want, it's more a matter of tolerances set at different levels, depending on where you've currently progressed in life. Perhaps Generation X, for example, simply has more to lose by outwardly rebelling.

In the UK, the laws of supply and demand have resulted in a property boom. As a result, baby boomers are comparatively less likely to be sustenance driven, are still concerned with outer-directed needs, yet have the luxury, time, and space to pursue an inner-directed path (hence the rise in so-called spiritual tourism and the self-development industry targeted at this group). They're also living a lot longer than their parents' generation.

There's growing evidence that Generation X, following a lengthy obsession with sustenance and outer-directed needs (the product of the late 1980s and 90s), may well be leading the charge toward alternative, ethical lifestyles and family-friendly ways of working, motivated by the delayed but recent baby boom within their ranks. This will undoubtedly have an important impact on the employment and purchasing decisions of this vital group, certainly within the important and trend-setting UK market.

In counterpoint, the lack of corporate loyalty within Generation Y is, to a large extent, buoyed by the relative financial security of their parents, more universities, comparatively high further education attendance levels, and a resultant, largely false sense of inferred status. Combine this with a "moregeoisie" (a term used by Tim Lott in *The New Middle Classes* on BBC4: "The children of Thatcher and Blair don't want to be middle class, they just want more stuff ... I call them the moregeoisie") obsession with brands that emphasizes the conspicuous physical manifestations of wealth, and the increasing complexity of influencing internal audiences becomes very clear. How do you talk in one voice to this lot? Cascade communication anyone?

In the UK, access to wealth and issues like housing supply and demand will bring future complications, but social commentators are observing that this should place greater pressure on maintaining relationships within families to secure inherited lines of income and ultimately focus on higher order needs. However you look at it, the internal and external brand battlegrounds of the future are fast moving to the higher ground of self-actualization. Brands will increasingly need to cater for higher order needs and to embrace values like authenticity in how they communicate.

There's little doubt that the realm of self-actualization is where the brand battles of the future will be fought and the combatants will need to tap into far more potent weapons than PR, glitz, cascade, volume, and spin. The brightest chief engagement officers will already have had the epiphanic revelation that employee engagement and customer satisfaction are eternally entwined and will have started to reengineer their communication processes accordingly. As you can't find just one way to talk to this audience, listen and get them talking to each other. They like it.

But back in the realm of the current: cascade-dominated, alignment-obsessed communication inevitably gives rise to systematic information spoon-feeding sessions colored by creative flashes. At least the obligatory slogan-splashed mouse mat, briefing pack, and suite of tactical communication tools are keeping so-called "Mac jockeys" busy in design houses, when the communication creativity goes into the design and creative platform rather than the strategy and approach. But going "wow" at a clever piece of design doesn't drive lasting engagement (we all get bored with our toys shortly after Christmas).

The communicator's role is extremely complex today. How do you encourage a consistent culture of customer service when one generation has been taught that the customer is always right, while the other considers themselves above deferential customer service roles because they're largely deluded about their own status? The answer can't possibly come from centralized communication, and, once again, calls for effective leadership at the supervisory level, where the motivation of the local ceo is tempered by experience, perspective, and responsibility. In this scenario, it is all the more important that the organization's values are explicit, the business goals are clear, the culture is well communicated, and the people processes are transparent. Alignment may be wrong, even impossible, but anarchy is from the same stable. After all, the organization is paying employees to represent it.

In a world where moregeoisie values dominate and have sadly become the prevailing order of the antiestablishment establishment, the pursuit of higher order needs is far from an effete plea. Are we entering an age when values, ethics, and spirituality are becoming the new iconoclasm, the contemporary punk?

I believe we are, but the leadership role models are taking their time to step forward. Bridget McIntyre, Royal & SunAlliance's UK chief executive, has gone out on a high-profile limb with her "Love the customer" campaign and has famously vowed to bring out the color and emotion in her people, in an attempt to inspire closer relations between customers and the brand. She's not only battling a masculine culture but is deliberately provoking perceptions, and it will be fascinating to see how she manages to develop a truly inspiring engagement program that doesn't become consigned to a legacy of workbooks, mouse mats, and mugs in the ultimate reactionary industry. Vivienne Cox, BP's executive VP of gas, power & renewables and its highest ranking woman, not only famously favors avant-garde design in her office furnishings, as a further expression of her true personality, and champions creative approaches to skills development but is also consciously portrayed as someone who balances the demands of work and family and who rates empathy as a key leadership trait. Some of the signals are encouraging.

Bridget's organization, Royal & SunAlliance (RSA), a 300-year-old brand, is serious about becoming the leading player in its crowded market and it's heartening to see that not only has it made the commitment to contemporize its image but it has made the link between employees, brand, and customer service. Through initiatives like "A great place to work" (GPTW), it is acknowledging the power of employee engagement.

GPTW is linked to a clear business case. For example, in its contact centers, its aim is to bring the "Love the customer" rallying cry to life by converting colleagues into fans, so that:

- people want to join
- they're allowed to express their commitment to customers
- they finish each conversation feeling good
- they develop the professional mastery to spot and deliver breakthrough customer value
- they receive upper quartile reward for performance
- they're supported by colleagues and technology that enable "efficient, perfect and now" service.

In the contact centers, RSA started by engaging staff in two-way communication and, as an output of the consultation stage, defined what it calls "the big five" components of the job that most drive satisfaction. The list has cross-generational appeal:

- base pay/bonus
- recognition
- work challenge and development
- flexible working environment
- physical working environment.

Given the growing discontentment with call centers generally, the opportunity is certainly there to make a difference. The engaging, emotive, ground-upwards approach is definitely impactful and brave, but the proof will be in the engagement and the implementation. To date, implementation has been fast-tracked in certain pilot centers, where the program has included:

- creation and training of a support team of local champions
- feedback and planning workshops led by employees
- local implementation of quick wins resulting from the above
- a commitment from the leadership to tackle the big five issues
- a range of employee recognition awards and forums
- launch of a new UK learning and development site
- careers workshops
- reviews of on-phone, off-phone time in search of balance
- flexible working contract reviews
- creation of chill-out rooms
- new refreshment suppliers
- renewed focus on social activity.

After 18 months, pilot centers are claiming positive employee feedback, true engagement, and promotions for key staff champions. In hard data terms, the results are:

- improved results across the board on the staff engagement survey
- attrition rates significantly reduced
- improved absence rates
- increased sales performance
- extensive external recognition
- reported total savings to the business of nearly £7 million (US$14 million).

This example of the power of engagement may focus on the call center environment but, like it or not, this really has become the pivotal customer contact point for most service industries now. It's reassuring, therefore, to see engagement activity prioritized in this way by enlightened leaders. However sophisticated and mature the internal audience may consider themselves to be, the principles of respect, empowerment, involvement, and two-way communication apply, as does the need to find engaging ways to close the relationship gap between organizational and individual values.

Turning the spotlight on the consumers where the storytelling is amplified, those who manage brands are often responsible for a form of cultural neurosis, due to consumer misunderstandings that arise from the mismatch between the promises that brands make and the actual needs they address. One of the difficulties in a society dominated by consumerism is the representation (whether premeditated or implied) that conspicuous consumption and indeed conspicuousness can be the ultimate satisfier of higher order needs.

Society can become obsessed with deficiency rather than growth needs. Most societies may have advanced beyond what Maslow referred to as physiological and safety stages, but many are now obsessed with esteem at the expense of qualities like love, belonging, and certainly self-actualization.

I believe that a new form of consciousness is awakening in both consumer and employee groups alike, linked to higher order values inherent in movements which have been around for some time like corporate social responsibility, ecological awareness and the green agenda but are currently flourishing. At a personal level this is translating into increased demand for roles that "make a difference," at both an economic and a social level.

It's easy to tell how deeply people feel about these values because they're quick to criticize organizations who are cynically attempting to jump on the bandwagon with thinly applied spin in advertising and empty boasts about their environmental credentials. Until you can back up claims with real behavior change, driven from within, my humble advice is "save your money" or you're only going to damage your brand further.

As employees and consumers shuffle up our collective hierarchy of needs, the challenge for brands becomes a new wave of opportunities based upon demand driven by heartfelt and extremely powerful values, which impact at an individual and national – or even a global – level.

THE NATIONAL PERSPECTIVE: NATION BRANDING

Recent research in the UK suggests that, whatever the dominant drivers, and despite the consumer frenzy, certain national brands, like brand Britain, are suffering in the wake of commercial brand mania.

Many believe that Britain is on a depressing downward spiral, according to polls by YouGov amongst others. Despite growing personal affluence, many Britains are ashamed of their national identity blaming immigration, "yobbishness", bad manners in customer service interactions and generally an absence of respect. There's evidence of a growing gap between optimism about personal prospects and pessimism about the state of the nation. In the YouGov poll, family comes top of the determinants of happiness.

This isn't just a British phenomenon, because with increasing mobility, better education and so on, the brand hierarchy is starting to adopt a more fluid structure. Are we witnessing a phenomenon where corporate brands are overtaking national brand identity in the hierarchy of consumers' consciousness?

These are worrying times for the custodians of nation branding are they not?

There is a clear relationship between the "feel-good" factor associated with the positive representation of the national brand and individual wellbeing, which has been proven to result in a positive impact on business and the economy. Think of international sports tournaments like the various World Cup events or the Olympic Games – examples of where corporate brands and national brands exist in a temporary but powerful patriotic symbiosis. Isn't it the dream of every politician to ride the crest of the feel-good wave more regularly? I've worked closely with the team who were behind much of the successful London 2012 Olympic bid. They acknowledge that a key point of difference between London's offering and its competitors was the emphasis placed on humanistic values rather than purely commercial imperatives, the focus on the Olympic ideals and delivering a games to engage future generations, to create a lasting legacy.

It is clear that, as in this example, governments are starting to have to take brand management principles increasingly seriously when attempting to manage national reputation and image, both to boost the balance of trade and to deal with internal confidence and self-image issues, which, if left unnurtured, will increasingly give rise to social disorder. Nation branding is becoming more important within and beyond national borders as it impacts on GDP. But I would argue, however, that the answer to national wellbeing doesn't rest solely on the shoulders of the government.

Corporate and national brands don't exist in parallel universes. The commercial success of corporate brands is tied to the prevalent Zeitgeist of the national markets in which they operate and vice versa. As a result, our brand decisions have far-reaching implications for the organizations we buy from and work for, and what we do while we're working there has an increasingly profound impact as well.

It's incumbent upon all of us to understand the relationship between brand categories, to uncover the sublime factors at work, because it's in our best interests. This cause and effect relationship should be a clarion call for brand managers, not least because it holds an important key to effective employee engagement.

Is managing a country brand like managing a company brand?

India has experienced a well publicized commercial boom in recent years. I have had the good fortune to visit India a couple of times on business recently and on one trip I was invited to participate in a series of discussions and debates about the relative brand positioning of a number of corporate and product brands. I also had the opportunity to participate in the brand India debate, a dialogue about developing and managing an endorsed brand for India, undertaken in the context of the growth in and globalization of the Indian economy.

As ever, I was struck, first and foremost, by India the country, as I traveled to four different cities in as many days. For those who've yet to visit, there's a reason why everything that has been written about India, from E. M. Forster to V. S. Naipaul, can't fail but convey the all-out assault on the senses that India represents. What a place to do business!

Having been whirled by smiling, friendly faces from airport to sumptuous hotel, from exquisite restaurant to ancient cab and then onto a heaving, dusty road, the trip to a technology business park in Bangalore was like a journey through time and back again. Once through the security perimeter, we quickly exchanged the congested anarchy, where brand new Mercedes dodge cows, carts and ruts in equal measure, for the familiar tokens and trappings of universal corporate culture. Name badges, dark business suits and on-brand architecture were the precursors to the brand experience walkthrough by our Infosys hosts, where impeccably polite, slick and well-tutored employees guided us through the journey of the evolution of their company, from legacy through to mission, with remarkable grace. Here was a country within a country, a corporate brand turned micro-society.

The brand India debate, hosted by the India Brand Equity Fund (IBEF) and facilitated by the Boston Consulting Group, was undertaken in Infosys's state-of-the-art, UN-style debating chamber. The key objectives of the IBEF were listed as:

- Promote "Made in India" as a brand in the overseas market
- Provide a forum in which a vision of India as a reliable global player is conceived, developed and disseminated
- Project India as a reliable supplier of world-class goods and services
- Guide industry in identifying and pursuing strategies and measures for promoting India's image.

In short, the objective was to develop an appropriate strategy for promoting India as a national brand and as a platform for the subsequent emergence of key Indian brands, like Titan Industries, the leading manufacturer of watches and jewelry, and other parts of the Tata Group, Jet Airways and so on, on the international brandscape. The forum included senior representatives from many of India's most respected institutions, professional services firms and organizations. The debate was preceded by a film intended to summarize India's perceived position on the world brandscape, the scale of the opportunity, the strengths and competitive threats (most notably that of its neighbor, China).

The film was something of a brand enigma for me. I found myself staring at a familiar succession of images, phrases, and dramatic motifs that brought the traveling experience and my agenda into stark relief. This wasn't a debate about brand India at all, it should have come with the equivalent of a government health warning: "Brand alignment can seriously damage your health!"

What was happening at a national scale echoed what I had seen at a corporate level, namely that rather than focus on authenticity, to embrace spirituality and diversity as well as stress compliance with international standards, talk of the brand was obsessed with the notion of "a land of contradictions which buyers don't understand or necessarily trust." The debate was far from appreciative and unfortunately was dominated by what brand India wasn't when compared to their Western competitors, rather than celebrating their differentiating essence. It was a classic case of cultural convergence and was more a rite of passage than a statement of strategic differentiation.

But for a number of obvious racial characterizations, the film we watched could have been overdubbed with American accents and reshown as a corporate video in any US technology company.

The debate that followed revolved around the metaphors of corporate cliché and was strangely characterized by an overriding lack of confidence. Yet the eminent people involved in the debate should have been buoyant, as the products and services represented by the assembly were truly groundbreaking, innovative and clearly commercially successful.

There were two glaring omissions from the discussion:

1. An innate lack of confidence in the relative commerciality of their businesses on the international stage (Titan, for example, makes some phenomenal products, including what was, at the time, the world's most slimline wristwatch and has skills, innovation, and technology to be proud of).
2. A failure to recognize that a national characteristic, an Indian authenticity, could be a formidable unique selling point (USP).

The pattern repeats itself at a national level, namely the obsession with logo and tag line, looking correct and addressing the rational trappings of brand development rather than unpacking the behavioral and, in this case, the spiritual dimension. The video had been slickly edited and produced and yet the Indian personality had been removed from it, rather like an eccentric relative who is escorted into the garden when the doorbell rings.

The process of understanding and defining national or country branding is clearly reliant upon the ability to discern those characteristics that are beneficial to specific commercial ends, like the ability to win more investment business, and then to attempt to nurture those characteristics. The proud goal should be to display a "made in" tag on products and services, to have attained the confidence to know that businesses will consistently deliver against the brand promise and that the quality of delivery will be a powerful marketing tool in its own right. This inevitably means that the country brand must carry the appropriate associations and these are inevitably linked to commercial factors that influence the ability to deliver, like industrial relations, political stability, trustworthiness and, increasingly, ethics and the national equivalent of corporate social responsibility.

Clearly, very few of those participating in the debate were willing to take the risk of proudly slapping a "Made in India" label on their products at that time. Rather than celebrate and accentuate the "Indian-ness" of their brands, they were obsessed with vanilla branding and emphasizing their ability to adopt Westernness. This made for a complicated debate about the national brand, as it's the very "other-ness" of India that is its core USP.

As Sunil Khilnani reiterates in *The Idea of India* (2003), India is an exceptionally diverse nation. Nation branding is complex regardless of this fact, because if it's going to transcend the logo and tag line compulsion, it involves bringing together extremely volatile stake-holder groups with varied emotional connections to the subject matter. I believe that the fear of embracing the diversity of stakeholder opinion can easily result in cultural schizophrenia unless a truly engaging and inclusive process is undertaken. This can result in brand schizophrenia and threatens to undermine the permanent offshoring of contact center facilities, for example. Difficulties in this aspect of the customer service industry haven't arisen for want of effort, but a lack of clarity about respective values, behaviors, strengths, and expertise has been behind soaring levels of customer complaints and threatens to damage both the corporate brands involved and the national brands themselves.

Indian tourism figures have shown around a 15 percent year-on-year growth in visitor numbers and it is clear that the spiritual dimension, ancient culture, and vibrancy are some of the key reasons why travelers favor India as a destination. Rather than embrace and promote this spiritual dimension, their senior business leaders were largely ignoring it and, in the process, were obsessed with aligning their business, products, services, and people with a cultural and business model that can never be more than a pale, if lower cost, version of their brand icons.

An obsession with the development of what some may see as the basic or foundational characteristics, such as safety and trustworthiness, is understandable, whether the brand in question is a product, a corporate or a country, but this shouldn't be at the expense of the core USP. The risk is that glory and tragedy are only a flip of the same coin away, and unless both dimensions are understood as part of a brand strategy, the results are going to lack authenticity and competitive edge.

Much of the responsibility for the subjugation of brand India in favor of corporate brands has to lie at the door of certain ill-advised organization development professionals involved with the offshoring activity. Leaders of corporate brands who have approached the move with the mistaken belief that corporate brand characteristics outweigh national characteristics are frankly ill advised and, in my view, sadly exhibiting characteristics redolent of imperial India. The approach rides roughshod over the national USP and will, in my view, prove to be commercially flawed. It's no surprise that we've witnessed a U-turn in call center policy in some sectors and a deliberate marketing strategy by some organizations, like NatWest, aimed at capitalizing on the fact that they have only UK call centers.

It's also no surprise that the national press lose no opportunity to highlight isolated incidents of fraud and abuse of trust arising from the outsourcing and offshoring of service industry organizations, as national brands square up to each other. I don't believe that this is predominantly a reactionary move or a reflection of an innate opposition to diversity but rather a resentful response to the passive/aggressive absence of authentic brand communication that undermines staff and customers alike.

Many of the financial services organizations, in particular, labor under the misguided belief that customers simply won't notice and don't need to be troubled by the fact that their transaction is undertaken by a chain of service delivery operatives located around the globe, yet linked by technology and apparently by corporate brand ideology. But the fact is, particularly within service industries, customers certainly do notice. Customers don't mind and often like the diversity – but only when it works. Is it right that customers buy into the quintessentially English experience of a long-established home furnishings retail brand yet, once a buying decision is made, they are potentially exposed to the harsh reality of a disempowered, process-dominated, corporate and depersonalized offshore finance experience, which bears little relation to the brand promise?

How often will banking customers tolerate attempts by an offshore call center operative diligently trying to sell to them by remaining on-script, and on-brand, or attempt to resolve a complex financial issue that they are patently not sufficiently informed or empowered to deal with? It isn't the fact that the person at the other end of the line is of a different nationality that galls, it's the cost-cutting arrogance of the company testing the customer's tolerance under the misguided notion that its brand characteristics are all-pervading and will ensure customer and staff loyalty. This, again, is alignment thinking. It is unsustainable and this attitude ignores the dynamics required between country and corporate branding. A customer service landmine is primed to explode.

As with a corporate brand, in order to create an authentic branding strategy for a country that stands a chance of being engaging, there needs to be clear dialogue between all stakeholders. It's a lot easier said than done and therefore needs a well-defined imperative. These stakeholders include business, government, the arts, tourism organizations, media, and education but should also involve representatives of the Everyman community, much like a holistic corporate brand development exercise would.

This dialogue requires a form of corporate and national integration that isn't easy to leverage. Clarifying key issues is emotionally charged but ignoring them, as we've seen, can lead to a higher price downstream. This consultation allows the facilitators to gauge the broad spectrum of characteristics, strengths and weaknesses, aspirations, and perspectives of the national psyche. They are then well placed to consult key stakeholders abroad.

Having undertaken this diagnostic, it's time to develop a strategy based on a professional model for the brand and to ensure that this includes programs and campaigns to engage core audiences with the goals as well as tangible initiatives, developments, improvements, and early, confidence-building wins. The brand development process needs to be focused on pragmatism: "we're doing this for the following reasons and you can expect to be impacted in the following ways." These ways need to reference likely behavior change as well as the physical outputs. A forum or system for linking the various stakeholders and "champions" and sharing ideas and best practices is essential, just as you would establish a representative consultation and engagement body if this were a corporate brand development exercise.

Most important of all, given that this is highly emotive territory, is to recognize that authentic brand development comes from building the national brand from within, rather than attempting to instruct, inform or align from outside; a tricky task for brand agencies needing their "fix" of recognition. The brand has to appeal to the critical mass, yet allow room for debate, rebellion, involvement, exploration of alternatives, innovations, and dissent – the cornerstones of engagement and ownership. It takes special skills, however, to ensure that this process doesn't become design by committee.

One organization making significant international strides, especially in India, is the technology company ARM Holdings. It has grown from a small UK base (the legendary 12 men in a Cambridge barn) to world-beating status and has had to develop both corporate and international brand management sensitivities along the way. I've watched it develop and am still fascinated by how an organization of "tech-heads" is a leader in employee engagement and holds true to its founding values, its brand DNA. But ARM has a unique take on brand engagement and management, which, like its products, it literally develops from within.

Case Study
ARM HOLDINGS (UK BUSINESS OF THE YEAR 2006)

Most people around the world have heard of Pentium processors, could probably hum the advertising jingle and even point to the label stuck onto their laptop or PC. But advertising isn't everything.

You've probably never heard of it, but ARM Holdings, a UK company founded in 1990, is a dominant force in the semiconductor market, leading the way in handheld technology. It is in a slightly different market but apparently outsells Pentium at a ratio of about 10:1. You won't be aware of it but you already have an intimate relationship with it, as ARM products are likely to be in your bedroom, bathroom, children's nursery, and car.

When it began, the company was called Advanced RISC Machines Ltd, but it changed its name to ARM Ltd in 1998 and then to ARM Holdings after its successful IPO on both the London and Nasdaq exchanges. Headquartered in Cambridge, UK, ARM Holdings designs reduced instruction set computing (RISC) microprocessors, physical intellectual property and related technology and software and sells development systems to enhance the performance, cost-effectiveness, and power efficiency of high-volume embedded solutions. Applications include modems, automotive systems, smart cards, and digital video. ARM processors are in at least 90 percent of cell phones and in most types of innovative household gadgets. It estimates that, in 2006, 1.5 billion people (a quarter of the world's population) bought an ARM-powered product. ARM has achieved all this with virtually no public brand and very little marketing or advertising. It is simply a unique blend of technical excellence and a passionate belief in values-led leadership.

ARM has the quiet confidence to define itself as: "The architecture for the digital world." Quite a claim – but no one is disagreeing.

Bill Parsons is the senior leader who has been in charge of its people engagement strategy for many years. When I first worked with Bill, back in 2001, ARM employed around 450 people and the City talk about ARM Holdings plc included the fact that ARM entered the FTSE 100 in 2000 and grew revenue by more than 60 percent that year. Despite the deepest and longest recession ever in the semiconductor industry, it continued to grow fast (46 percent in 2001) and maintained operating margins of over 30 percent.

Even when ARM dropped out of the FTSE 100 due to the general sentiment toward high-tech stocks, it remained one of the few technology companies in the world that met or exceeded shareholder expectations each quarter. Yet it doesn't pin the medals on its exceptional ability to innovate alone.

The industry may have what some would call "an image problem" based around the cliché of a dysfunctional tech-head, inventing gadgets on his or her own in a darkened room. Perhaps surprisingly, however, Bill completely debunks the technical sociopath caricature with an amused laugh when you meet him.

Emotional intelligence is treasured at ARM and first and foremost, Bill puts ARM's exceptional performance fairly and squarely down to what he calls its social capital:

Communication, relationships and making connections is absolutely vital and has always been a strong point here. In fact it's where most of our innovation comes from. Rather than laboratories or darkened rooms, the Cambridge atrium has long been an important and symbolic social gathering point to celebrate success, face challenges and to share stories. It's a physical symbol of our partnership and people-first philosophy and the top team have always been accessible role models of this philosophy.

The Cambridge atrium isn't a lavish, over-engineered space, in fact it has the relaxed informality of a university common room, yet the multiplying massed ranks of empty vintage champagne bottles lining the walls, each commemorating a milestone in the company's history, are testimony to a great deal of hard but rewarding work.

As you would expect, ARM people are largely highly intelligent, questioning, even quietly cynical by nature; it goes with the territory.

The closest cultural comparison I can make is to that of the investment banks, where employees know that their organization attracts the best in their field, is assured in its technical ability and confidence blooms as a result. However, there certainly isn't the "alpha" competitive, boss-watching mentality at ARM. Because the internal culture matters so much, everybody takes responsibility for the contribution they make to that culture and they have had to work hard at maintaining relationships, particularly as they have grown.

They thrive on authentic communication grounded in their core values. You simply have to be able to match words with actions at ARM and, as a consequence, "sheep-dip" brand communication simply won't work with the ARM internal audience. It doesn't work with clients either, so it doesn't happen.

The ARM brand clearly radiates from all its leadership team, starting with Warren East, the CEO (ARM has only had two CEOs, Sir Robin Saxby, co-founder and Warren's predecessor, having become president of the Institute of Engineering and Technology while retaining a link with ARM as chairman emeritus). This isn't a business where presidential-style figureheads and mouthpieces thrive. So there's no arguing about window ratios or parking spaces among the top team. In fact, there's a legend that ARM has made 100 millionaires and that most of them still work there. You would never know it.

Despite major recessions in its key markets, and the disruptive effects of making a series of acquisitions that have given ARM significant presence in North America, Europe, the Middle East, Asia Pacific, and India, ARM declared total revenues of £263 million (US$447 million) in 2006 compared to £232 million (US$394 million) in 2005 and returned £89 million (US$151 million) in cash to shareholders through a share buyback program and dividends.

ARM is a successful, growing, global business, whichever way you look at it. But the growth hasn't been driven by advertising, it owes nothing to PR, and it isn't simply down to technological excellence.

Proud to call themselves "geeks," the senior management team, who clearly enjoy each other's company, are just as proud to attribute their success to core and fundamental people principles and a set of values that have stood the test of time. Mike Inglis, executive VP marketing, says:

Our model is that we have grown from the ground up. Despite the fact that I wasn't one of the original "12 men in a Cambridge barn," that pioneering spirit and the founding values are very much alive here. It comes across long before you join, largely in the behaviors of the people you meet during the recruitment process. Once you commit to join ARM, it's there in the way we talk to each other, the truly open door policy, our belief in getting out there to personally build bridges and spread the core DNA. I truly believe that, much more than anywhere else I've worked, it starts at the top but spreads like wildfire. As a top team, we can pretty much cover each other's jobs – I've seen the likes of IBM aspire to this model. I guess the big difference here is that there's no hint of it being a token, developmental thing or something we need to conscript people to do, we are genuinely happy to help out when needed and this brings out the best in colleagues.

ARM's leadership approach, like all the best people-centered things, is essentially simple. It is based upon a sound, clear model and an explicit set of values.

Leadership
The way we do things at ARM
Purpose, People, Process, Performance
"A special company of special people."

The ARM values
Deliver results
Teamwork and selflessness
Constructive proactivity
Partnership
Responsiveness

Bill Parsons calls the relationship between these elements "the glue," or more "geekily," "systems thinking." Bill believes that the people processes in the business should be considered in a systematic way, as they are all connected to deliver better bottom line performance. This approach may upset the so-called free-thinking creatives or more sensitive HR traditionalists who talk about hearts and emotions before minds, but I agree with Bill. In order to influence performance, it is important to take a disciplined approach to understanding and defining the core people processes, like recruitment, induction, performance management, skills development, and communication. Only then will it be possible to recognize the elements in the management mix that have the greatest impact on the bottom line by impacting the culture (the way we do things), and only then is it possible to pass on the skills required to engage leaders and employees alike with the people factors that most influence performance.

If you're ever in any doubt about which people processes should take priority, ask yourself what you would do in a startup situation where your bank account was providing the financing. ARM has managed to maintain that entrepreneurial mentality and, by focusing on systems thinking, it has found an authentic and appropriate way to engage with its core internal stakeholders. Bill Parson's systems thinking approach plays to his analytical audience, yet it is a core thesis running through this book, namely that joined-up thinking provides the framework within which authentic employee engagement thrives. Innovation and discipline are fine bedfellows.

Speaking to their senior leaders, they consistently attribute the company's continued success to two key factors:

1. Exceptional people, leading to exceptional innovation and performance.
2. An innate understanding of what we're about, our culture, the way we do things at ARM.

> "ARM will mean the best people, creating the
> most innovative solutions."
> *Statement of strategic intent, ARM board, 2003*

Critics will claim that it's comparatively easy to establish and reinforce a culture when the workforce is relatively small, stable, and comes from the same cultural roots. It's a while since the ARM demographic matched this profile and I would argue that parochialism carries its own stifling risks, were it not for the fact that the ARM workforce has changed dramatically in the last seven or so years. The demographic when it started was:

- 12 people, 1 site, 1 country
- 0% outside the UK
- average age 27

- 0% Asian origin
- 100% male
- 90% graduate
- $0 revenue/head
- 5 new people that year.

Compare that with the situation today:

- 1,600 people, 35 sites, 11 countries
- 60% outside the UK
- average age 37
- more than 30% Asian origin
- 84% male
- more than 90% graduate
- $330,000 revenue/head
- 400 new people this year.

Speaking to line managers within the business now, compared to four or five years ago, it's clear that the key group within the overall demographic is maturing in line with its shifting profile rather than just growing older together. To toy with the previous caricature, the culture today feels a bit like the shy teenage boy lured from the computer in his bedroom only to discover that he can now impress others with the skills and knowledge he's acquired because the rest of the world has woken up to the power of technology. Yes, geeks have become interesting, even sexy.

Within ARM, the technical specialists have had to ramp up their emotional intelligence, team development, mentoring, and all-important communication skills as they're needed to spread the ARM way of doing things within their expanding teams and across the globe. The employment brand is strong and the "ARM way" has become a term most people in the business will use instinctively at some stage in your conversation with them.

Yesterday's technicians are also today's line managers and, due to genuine affection for and belief in the business, they have chosen to stay at ARM and evolve their roles rather than seek out highly paid technical-specialist roles elsewhere (and there's little doubt that ARM personnel are in high demand). Not everyone makes the transition, some people just aren't cut out to be line managers and ceos, but the door remains open to them as ARM doesn't believe in an "up or out" approach to line management.

A combination of deep-seated loyalty, the widening availability of global responsibilities, and the fact that they have matured with the business (many having now started families) has seen the core management cadre evolve with the business. Their priorities have changed but the onus is still very much on performing for ARM, which in turn, delivers for them:

> The pressure has certainly changed here and we're increasingly regulated and driven by the demands of shareholders and the markets. It's easy to see bureaucracy as non-value-adding and it's certainly not something any of us relish, but this is still very much a sociable place and it's certainly the feedback I get from new entrants. Our conferences and twice-yearly parties used to be fairly singles dominated, but now that people bring their families there's a fresh dynamic. It's true to say that there's less of an incentive to stay late when you haven't yet heard your toddler's latest words. We just find different ways as a community to get the job done between us in the time available.

The line manager who gave this comment did mention that the definition of fun had certainly changed but that, on reflection, it wasn't anything to do with the leadership. In fact, the responsibility had now shifted to him and his peers to find fresh ways of invigorating the culture. Typically, this line manager had just been discussing this with one of the directors and they had agreed to explore the conversation at the next director's meeting. Do you know anywhere else where this type of relationship between senior management exists or where directors would take the trouble to talk about the fun factor at a board meeting?

The skills profile of a leader at ARM is perhaps surprisingly soft-skills focused:

People skills:
- Cares about people
- A mentor and continual coach

Team skills:
- Develops and enables the team
- Identifies skills holes in the team and fills them
- Focuses on leadership rather than hands on
- Empowers people and avoids micromanagement

Personal skills:

- Articulates the vision
- Passion and drive
- Makes tough decisions
- "Can do" problem solver
- Checks progress and balances
- Understands the technical issues.

This is hardly the profile of the techno-sociopath and its breadth places significant demands on the recruitment, induction, performance management, and development processes, which have all been carefully constructed to support and drive both performance and culture.

Its people policy outlines the expectations for managers within ARM. It defines the key duties and responsibilities for an ARM manager.

Everything of real value to our customers and shareholders produced by ARM comes from the people within the business. Exceptional results and performance are a product of the skills, abilities, creativity, knowledge and efforts of highly motivated employees.
Managers and leaders are responsible for ensuring we can all produce these sustainable results by harnessing and developing the individuals and teams within ARM. This policy simply sets down the ARM perspective on management responsibilities and the minimum expectations for managers. Training and development is provided to help all managers and leaders improve their capabilities.

Line managers are supported by a comprehensive organization development strategy and skills development program to help them make the most of the opportunities presented by growth.

ARM's key people processes consist of:

- Feedback and development system
- Talent assessment program
- Global learning and development team
- Technical development
- Management development
- Professional development
- Internal conferences to network and share ideas

- International assignments
- Succession planning.

The new additions to the ARM family all receive a comprehensive induction (the big picture) led by a senior leader, wherever they may be located. They are infusing the ARM culture with a diversity that has brought unexpected rewards. But like the best diversity approach, it's an inclusive, two-way process centered around a clear employment brand. ARM's values permeate the core of the business. They are the very essence of their employment brand and form the foundation for all key processes, from recruitment, through to induction, performance management and skills development (collectively known as the AFDS or ARM Feedback and Development System). They are the backbone behind the acquisitions and the bridge between the merging cultures.

> "With growth, ARM's regions will develop more
> defined identities while its people remain
> emotionally connected to the whole."
> *Statement of strategic intent, ARM board, 2003*

Unpacking the ARM values reinforces the focus on interpersonal skills:

- *Delivery of results* that benefit ARM – produces results that either benefit the whole or part of ARM, achieves the results by any acceptable means necessary, including innovation, own expertise, and using others' expertise
- *Teamwork and selflessness* – connected to the business, communicates openly, shares information and knowledge, networks internally and externally, persuades rather than pushes, involves colleagues, respects colleagues. Always thinks and acts for the company, the team, shareholders, and the customer ahead of themselves, works for the greater good of ARM – does not act selfishly or in own interest
- *Constructive proactivity* – develops practical solutions, takes leadership, has a "can do" rather than "won't do" approach, positive thinker, makes it happen, acts with a sense of urgency
- *Partner and customer focus* – an employee who is partner and customer (both internal and external) focused thinks and acts with the best interests of the customer, understands their needs, understands the strengths of ARM's business, and helps develop ARM business process and culture

- *Responsiveness* – always reacts quickly and with a sense of urgency to requests, issues, emails or other events in a timely and flexible fashion, based on consideration of the dependent needs of others.

As Bill Parsons says:

Our values form an important part of the due-diligence process when we're considering a significant structure change, like an acquisition, a key recruitment, or new partnership. Most organizations claim to do this but I can say "hand on heart" that one of our key considerations is how the two entities will complement each other and work together from a cultural and behavioral perspective and we place great emphasis on learning after each structure change. A great deal of time and effort is spent engaging our new team mates in the ARM way, our core values and why they're critical to our business. But we take an equally appreciative approach to how we engage existing employees with the skills and attributes we most value in our new colleagues, not just the hard-nosed equity.

Most importantly, from an internal brand perspective, communication is paramount as is the oft-repeated phrase: "an employee who is partner and customer focused thinks and acts with the best interests of the customer." The same standards are expected in relationships with external partners, a philosophy that is fundamental to the ARM operating model.

As we've seen and will see in other case studies, like the Zurich example, encouraging employees to blur the distinctions between customer and employee encourages empathy, stimulates innovation, and makes for a more engaging and ultimately rewarding workplace experience.

> "Continual self-betterment through reflection and feedback, coaching and mentoring, training and education, is the lifeblood of personal and organizational change. Through on-the-job and formal training we aim to promote and support the development of everyone both individually and in teams to achieve their potential, enhance their ARM adventure and enable them to contribute to the wider success of ARM. We will develop our leaders and managers as coaches who together help build a scalable and sustainable organization. ARM will create pace and passion by inspiring people to achieve more."
> *Statement of strategic intent, ARM board, 2003*

The ARM directors make the point quite explicitly that "Leaders at all levels are the key drivers of employee engagement at ARM." And in true systems-thinking fashion, they have studied the factors contributing to employee engagement and through regression analysis (they undertake regular employee surveys) are clear about the key drivers of employee satisfaction (which, incidentally, include the fun factor).

Having survived and thrived, despite the dark days for technology stocks, ARM has become a truly global company. It is the first to acknowledge that globalization brings its own challenges. But as ARM has grown, the leaders have been extremely concerned to ensure that they retain the equity inherent in their brand and culture. There's an understated Englishness about ARM that isn't self-effacing but is confident without being brash or effusive. To quote Bill Parsons again:

> Our intention has always been to listen first, to sell the ARM values and way of operating and to retain and reconfigure on the back of what's working, provided it fits with our core values. There have been examples where we've had to make significant changes at the top and in key management positions following an acquisition. We prefer to retain the local leadership but do believe in spreading the ARM DNA, which sometimes means international buddying opportunities for Cambridge employees. But we're increasingly adopting an approach of mentoring and developing local leaders, supported rather than supplanted by the UK team. Our core value of selflessness holds the key in this regard, as it's vital that the national characteristics of the ARM offices come to the fore, given that business is conducted very differently across the globe.

Interestingly, on the occasions when the UK board has had to introduce ARM appointments onto the management teams of its international companies, as they did with their recent US acquisition, they're usually senior support roles in areas like operations, finance, and HR, the traditional repositories for core people processes. Importantly, there is an insistence that people processes are synchronized the world over. At the forefront of these core people processes is communication. Summer Fern, communications adviser, explains:

> How we engage with our people the world over is absolutely vital and that means employing the full range of communication tools and techniques. We try hard to stay true in spirit to the intimacy of

the days when we could all shout across to each other or meet in the atrium even when that's not always practical.

It's clear that ARM has had to professionalize its communication processes as a way of ensuring that its network of employees is constantly engaged with the organization's values. After all, the senior leaders can't be everywhere at once.

Not everything is left to ebb and flow with the natural rhythms of human interaction. Systems thinking applies to communication as well, although some of you may be disappointed to hear that, surprisingly, ARM is not overreliant on podcasts, blogs, RSS and wikis and has yet to develop an online social network. They prefer to talk. As it has grown and the communication baton has had to pass from directors to line managers, ARM has "professionalized" its store of tools and channels. Elements of its communication strategy, called "Commitment to communication," include:

- ARM feedback and development system – the main one-to-one process
- AIM – monthly intranet newsletter
- "Lunch 'n' learns" – ad-hoc presentations on specific topics (technical and nontechnical)
- The (now legendary) organizational development conference
- Big picture inductions
- Top-level management's yearly meeting
- Surveys and focus groups
- Employee feedback mechanisms
- Directors Q&A (minimum twice per year) – executives visit each office to answer employee questions and engage in dialogue
- Team briefings/quarterly results – updates on the business and results
- Internal conferences – engineering and nontechnical
- Quarterly email from CEO – Warren's update.

Whether dealing with strategic partners within its market or the ARM offices themselves, its people-centered strategy calls for an inclusive approach that builds "from the ground up," not a blanket bombing of on-brand messages from the center.

ARM has taken the step of designing a bespoke intranet (courageous in an environment of technical whiz kids), with a dedicated manager; but it's very straightforward. More importantly, it has developed face-to-face briefing processes for line managers and supports them via a raft of people skills courses masterminded by Sara Feulner, their US-based HR Director and Sonia Bicknell, the dedicated director of learning and development, who says:

> I love working here as it's both a collegiate and challenging environment where the people keep me on my toes constantly. Despite finalizing my Ph.D. in this area, I'm constantly being questioned about any assumptions and as a consequence the development solutions we offer have to be extremely pragmatic, tailored and deliver results. ARM employees take little at face value and only truly engage if they can see the benefits and have the chance to explore both theory and practice. All our work has the core values at its heart, which helps to ensure immediacy and relevance. The directors have extremely demanding travel schedules and yet they can't be in all places all of the time, which puts added responsibility on our line managers to become the next generation of key communicators, beyond their immediate teams and this doesn't always come naturally to technical specialists.

While growth has demanded that face-to-face communication has a deal more structure to drive consistency of key messages, skills development backup and measurement to ensure quality, and a clear story running through everything, informality is still treasured and is seen as the best way of ensuring dialogue.

ARM is not a business that flashes its brand like heraldic adornments. For ARM, the whole is better than the sum of the parts (think cell phone, where the ARM component is key but only one link in the customer service chain). Out there in the customer sphere, ARM promotes what it calls the "ARM connected community": "A community of leaders and visionaries enabling the digital world."

ARM is acutely conscious that it is now a global organization and while it desperately wants to retain the founding intimacy of its leafy Cambridge hub, it needs to make its communication as relevant to someone turning up to work in Silicon Valley as to their bustling Bangalore counterpart.

Despite the legendary stories, despite the folklore about a business based on 12 men in a barn, ARM simply wouldn't have achieved what it has and be as confident as it is about the future if it was solely reliant upon hero leaders to engage its staff. Its success depends entirely upon spreading its ARM DNA confidently but respectfully.

Speaking to the line management community, it's clear that this is an important stage in the evolution of ARM and, inevitably, a few growing pains are setting in. The company demographic and low staff attrition has meant relative stability without becoming stale, but:

- how does it keep the culture fresh?
- how does it continue to embrace diversity?
- how does it ensure that it retains its core?

Bill Parsons says:

As we've grown, we've all had to develop different competencies and within our industry, growth has meant increasing bureaucratization which could stifle our ability to innovate, if we let it. This is contributing to a sense that we're perhaps not always having as much fun as we used to.

As "fun" is proven to be one of the key drivers of employee engagement at ARM, it is given due respect, as is any feedback suggesting that the "fun factor" may be at risk. "Fun has always been the oil in the ARM machine, a sort of informal core value" and it has always placed great stock in providing opportunities for people to make connections with each other. It has maintained the tradition of the Christmas party and summer barbeque, when these have fallen out of favor elsewhere, and when the balance sheet was under pressure. In addition, ARM has traditionally placed great store in its global conferences (GOCs), which have been opportunities for 50–70 of its top performers to meet and network around a loosely structured, network based framework.

Bill says:

We haven't been as diligent with our conferences as we could have been recently, partly out of a desire not to be seen to be too Cambridge-centric and partly because our feet have hardly touched the ground. GOCs will evolve into becoming increasingly subject-focused in future and we'll work hard to ensure that they are globally inclusive.

But the secret of maintaining the intimacy that underpins true engagement at ARM probably won't be driven from the top. As Bill says:

We're constantly reviewing our communication and engagement

strategy in light of feedback from our people, and there will be new initiatives like the increasing use of webcasts and video conferencing when actual face-to-face communication of key messages simply isn't possible. Senior leaders aren't any good to anyone if their home lives are wrecked by our schedules. What we won't compromise on, though, is the commitment of our top team to employee engagement and no amount of technology can replace the intimacy of connecting with people in person. We'll keep working on finding new ways.

What the ARM Holdings case illustrates quite clearly is that the key to maximizing returns from the relationship between national and corporate branding comes down to two key things:

1. Absolute clarity about what the respective brands stand for.
2. Mutual respect for the importance of culture and values and a willingness to evolve the common ground.

ARM's India office is likely to become its largest employee base in the very near future but India's relationship with the ARM HQ is based upon symbiosis rather than any hint of cultural colonialism. The business has ensured that the Indian operation embraces the core ARM values and is embracing and respecting what the Indian business has to offer in turn. It isn't re-creating Cambridge in Bangalore.

It's no surprise that, in a field open to businesses from all sectors, in November 2006, ARM was chosen as the UK Business of the Year at the National Business Awards. It was assessed against criteria that included leadership, innovation, growth, and financial return. Also in November 2006, it was given the accolade of "the company with the greatest capacity to innovate" in the *Management Today* awards for Britain's Most Admired Companies, and in January 2007, it won the pan-European Union award as European Business of the Year. I'll let Mike Inglis have the last word:

Our achievements prove the value of a brand strategy based upon how things get done rather than the noise we make in the market. First and foremost, we have good products that work. It's a relatively simple formula at ARM, the customer, partner and people experience is what shapes our brand.

SUMMARY OF KEY LEARNINGS

- Authentic brands aren't about promises made but promises delivered
- Individuals ultimately control brands through their values-based decisions
- The modern obsession with conspicuous individualism is gradually giving way to global consciousness and responsibility
- Push communication isn't engagement, which appeals to higher order needs and motivations
- Leaders must be the owners and architects of culture change and have themselves to be engaged with the goals and ambitions first
- Nation branding is growing in importance but is more than a logo and tag line
- The story is an ancient and powerful engagement tool and story-telling an innate skill
- Systems thinking is key to balancing people-centered, enabling activity and business results

5 Things to Try Today

1. Measure customer and employee brand perceptions regularly but focus twice as much attention on values and behaviors than on the physical and process elements of the brand.
2. Carry out a values audit and chart the relationships between values and the brand.
3. Find ways to link brand engagement activity to the bottom line.
4. Take an inclusive and involving approach to developing the story about the relationship between the brand and the vision.
5. Ensure that the brand is embedded in all key people processes.

ACT 3

THROUGH THE LOOKING GLASS

Now, if you'll attend, Kitty, and not talk so much, I'll tell you all my ideas about Looking-glass House. First there's a room you can see through the glass – that's just the same as our drawing room, only the things go the other way.

"They don't keep this room so tidy as the other," Alice thought to herself, as she noticed several of the chessmen down in the hearth among the cinders.

Through the Looking Glass and What Alice Found There (Lewis Carroll, [1872], 1998 edition)

JULY 1996

It's a Friday night; it's been a tough month. Everyman has taken his new team out for the night to celebrate the successful delivery of the pitch document. There have been the usual pressure-driven squabbles but he's struck by how well they all get on, once through the revolving door and guards are lowered. Morale's been a bit tricky just lately so they could really do with nailing this project but judging by the team creative meeting, there's a lot to be cheerful about. The weekend starts here!

Conversation is bubbling tonight, always does once the deconstruction of the events of the working week has been dealt with and the more serious heads have politely done their duty and then disappeared for the night. It turns out that their latest recruit has been keeping a few secrets. She's a relatively shy and retiring soul by day, but, as it turns out, runs an outdoor pursuits center at the weekends, training expedition leaders. Who would ever have guessed? She's volunteered to run next week's talkback session for the senior account managers.

He's feeling fairly fit at the moment, despite their hectic social calendar and workload. This is going to be his last season as club captain but he's working hard with his coach to make sure it's a good year at the club. To be truthful, the social scene is having a serious impact on relations at home and people are starting to ask sarcastic questions at work when he disappears for another social tournament (and to think he only took up golf again for the business networking).

As he finishes his beer and tries to attract the barman's eye, the lights from a passing car catch his attention and he looks up to see a new Audi convertible drive past the window. He looks on admiringly, but forlornly, as they're not on the managerial grade car list.

Thoughts drift to home. They have the three-bedroom house in a good area, two holidays a year, all the latest gadgets, and a group of friends who keep them on their toes at dinner parties. "Just a shame the job's become such a drag. Some people must get used to the routine, the travel, the rituals but it feels like I'm going through the motions," he thinks to himself. He calls to the barman, orders another round for the troops and returns to his seat next to Ms Career Path.

On his way home, there's a delay on the line. Apparently an old guy in a worn bowler hat and dark suit, clearly the worse for wear, has been abusing fellow passengers, "mooing" at them like a cow and shouting through tears of laughter "40 years, 40 years" while throwing papers from his briefcase into the air like a dipsomaniac guest at a filing clerk's wedding. Now he's chanting the same line Everyman vaguely recognizes from some TV cowboy series "moving, moving, moving, keep those people moving ...," as he paces up and down the serried lines of irritated, slightly scared, but mildy amused commuters "Mad old loser. How would you get into such a state? Now I'm going to be in even more trouble at home."

While the train waits for the backlog to clear, he phones his partner. She said something this morning about taking a sabbatical and as they're going to be stuck here some time ...

Act 3 is all about perceptions, connections and communication. Internal communication has long been perceived as the poor relation of marketing and yet it's time the prodigal son of the communications mix was given a place at the top table. But if the profession is going to make it there and justify a place, it's going to have to demonstrate mastery of the full range of connectivity, from tactical information push all the way through to stakeholder engagement. It's also going to have to consistently exhibit the general leadership skills expected of fellow professionals. It's a tough ask.

Lack of coordination in internal communication is a problem because it undermines the consistency on which a brand depends. (Quirke, 2000)

There's definitely a compelling business case for greater professionalism and the opportunity certainly exists to elevate the status of internal communication; but how to get there? I believe that key to this potential elevation will be the act of finally and justifiably taking the high ground in the battle for authentic employee brand engagement, before someone else does.

Internal communication should, quite frankly, be leading the internal brand engagement charge, for as we've explored, brands are simply empty promises to customers unless employees are engaged enough to deliver against those promises consistently and enthusiastically. And the internal communication profession should be all about engagement. But employees are nothing if not demanding internal customers and there's also the small matter of carving out some space in which to grow.

WHAT'S BEEN HAPPENING IN THE COMMUNICATION MARKET?
In conversation with an industry expert

Mandy Thatcher is head of content at Melcrum and is responsible for researching customer needs and sourcing articles, case studies, and news that cover emerging trends and topics. Mandy joined Melcrum in 2002 as the editor of *Strategic Communication Management* and before that edited a number of trade publications, including *Marketing Business* and *Sales Promotion*. As someone who has looked into the communication looking glass from both sides, she's extremely well informed about developments and trends concerning the key disciplines within the engagement mix.

Melcrum is a research and training business, with a long-established and growing international reputation as an important player in the internal communication market. In many respects, it is one of the first hybrid corporate/social networking pioneers and through its global networks, it connects nearly 20,000 (and growing) professional communicators in sharing what works.

Melcrum's international research spans industries, is well respected within the communication market, and sets out to constantly probe and evaluate the link between communication and the bottom line, whether through improving the communication skills of leaders and managers; getting the most from new technologies; engaging employees through strategy communication; getting change communication right; or proving the value of what communicators do through effective research and measurement.

IB: How would you compare and contrast the internal communication profession now, compared to, say, five years ago?

MT: As you know, we undertake regular research into trends within the internal communication market and, more to the point, our key players mix with professionals within this business all the time (I've just got back from our US conference event, in fact, and our Australasia event takes place later this year). It's taken a while but there's certainly more of a sense now of the profession being recognized as a discipline in its own right, rather than just an offshoot of HR, PR or marketing.

IB: From what I've experienced, there appears to be a growing differentiation between internal communication and engagement. They are actually different milestones on the same journey and, in my view, the entire gamut should form part of the remit of internal communication.

MT: Interestingly, the primary responsibility for employee engagement initiatives (including industrial relations, union negotiations, and formal consultation), increasingly rests with HR, but some of the elements are also frequently shared between a number of other "people" functions.

The clear trend is for internal communication to be sited a step away from the CEO and positioned in either corporate communication or HR. Both provide an opportunity to build a more powerful, joined-up proposition – whether as part of an integrated communication strategy within corporate communications or an employee engagement strategy within HR.

I think the big difference is down to the fact that more leadership teams acknowledge that employees who understand the business strategy and feel some sense of commitment to making it happen are central to business success. That's had a positive impact on the status and credibility of the profession over the past five years, because internal communication can play a big role in both helping employees understand the business strategy, and helping them feel connected to the business on a more emotional level.

So in organizations where internal communicators are ready to take up the challenge, they're gradually being given the opportunity to shape the way strategy is communicated and coach leaders and managers to help them become better communicators too. But in many other organizations, leaders either haven't recognized the potential of the function, or the communicators themselves haven't made the journey from tactician to strategist and simply aren't ready to play a more influential role in the business [see Figures 3.1 and 3.2].

IB: So the data suggest that the power struggle between internal communication and marketing appears to have shifted to include HR in the mix. This certainly seems to be echoed in the recruitment market, where what are called "senior employee engagement roles" are advertised as part of the HR portfolio. It's clear to me that the technical aspects of this specialism are still evolving (there are training courses in internal communication springing up everywhere), but a fair proportion of the people who work within the profession haven't necessarily adapted as rapidly to meet the challenge of change, they haven't arrived at that stage in what you describe as "the journey." You run regular international conferences and seminars catering to this audience; how have the participants changed over the years?

	2003 %			2006 %
Corporate communication	28	↑	+16%	44
PR/public affairs	15	↓	–7%	8
Marketing	15	↓	–6%	9
Office of the CEO	12	↓	–8%	4
HR	8	↑	+10%	18
Strategy and planning	4			2
Organizational development	2			2
Legal and corporate affairs	2			1
Finance	0.5			1
Other	13			9

FIGURE 3.1 **Where the internal communication function sits (all data)**

Source: The Pulse © Melcrum Publishing, 2006

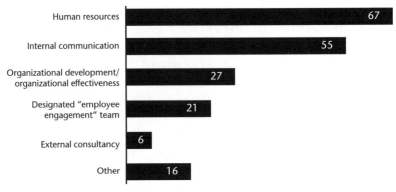

FIGURE 3.2 **Function responsible for overseeing employee engagement (all data; those with a formal engagement program)**

Note: Percentages do not equal 100 because respondents could select more than one function.

Source: Employee Engagement © Melcrum Publishing, 2005

MT: I think the dichotomy between tactician and strategist is becoming more noticeable. There's certainly nothing wrong with practitioners who are more focused on tactical stuff like managing the intranet or editing the employee newsletter and if this is what their leadership demands of them and they enjoy these roles, then it makes sense for them to become real specialists in terms of delivery. But there are an increasing number of practitioners who really want to make a difference inside their organizations and be taken seriously. They're the people at conferences and training workshops who expect to take something useful back to the office, who are constantly building the business case for more resources, more respect, and more influence.

IB: I would argue that it's in the interest of the profession that differentiation starts to filter in, as the profession needs to be more assertive in structuring expectations. It's quite clear to me that there are essentially two tiers of internal communicators right now:

- *Tier one* – who largely come from senior management stock, may have agency or consultancy experience, probably have experience in business roles beyond the communication disciplines, control their own budgets and develop a strategy and business case and set their own measurement, are comfortable at both the tactical and strategic level, and have credibility at a senior level because they understand how business works.

- *Tier two* – who are enthusiastic, skilled tactical practitioners and contribute to strategy, probably have a technical communication specialism, have some budgetary control, some supervisory experience, have a passion for gathering and distributing content, and largely access senior leaders through a senior line manager or boss.

Although clients fall into both categories, we mostly work with what I call tier one communication professionals when assisting with major change initiatives like new strategy, culture or brand development programs. It tends to be a different client profile when helping with tactical communication development and design. The differences are accentuated when the worlds merge or when the communication brief shifts from pushing messages to eliciting real engagement. For example, we were recently called in at short notice by a well-known retailer to help with a communication challenge. It was during the festive run-in, a critical period for retailers, and the company was caught between needing to renegotiate employee terms and conditions on the one hand and the unions and employee resistance on the other. The situation would not have arisen had its internal communication function focused less on pushing messages through inappropriate channels and more on achieving true engagement. There was a happy ending but it was a close call and has resulted in the recruitment of a tier one communicator, independent from, but coordinating with, HR.

Would you say that this is a UK issue or have you've detected any international differences in approach across key markets?

MT: We hold events and offer training in Europe, the US, and Australia at present (the latter covering the Asian market), and the challenges faced by practitioners in all these areas remain fairly consistent, particularly among those from large corporations, where the corporate brand often takes precedence over nationality. The most obvious differences are in the delivery of solutions. Communication styles and techniques are clearly more successful if they are pitched at the right level and conform to the cultural norms and expectations of the country in which they're delivered. Strategies are similar, but delivery varies depending on the proficiency of the communicator and the cultural demands of the country.

IB: That certainly maps to the experience of communication professionals developing and implementing engagement strategies for global organizations. We recently carried out international research for our client at Shell and were struck by how the issues and concerns for employees in the UK, the US, Asia, and Central and Eastern Europe varied so significantly. In Asia and the US, for example, there was high demand for communication from the very top, whereas this is waning in appeal in the UK and is now cynically received in Eastern Europe, where they place primary stock in local community-based communication. A consistent appeal across markets, however, was for a map to be drawn up showing links between the internal communication disciplines, whether within HR, marketing, change or internal communication, which would give a clear and consistent picture and story and could be adapted by local communicators for local markets.

Visualizing the volume of communication traffic is one technique for appreciating the scale of congestion in the metaphoric airways that many communicators have to face up to. Air traffic control is therefore a major issue with companies of this size, particularly during times of change and where every associated project seems to have a communication launch pad. Internal politicking rears its head when trying to address issues like ownership and prioritization. How do you think internal communication practitioners match up to their fellow communication colleagues?

MT: I edited a journal for marketing professionals about five years ago and many of the conversations I heard in the industry at that time were similar to those I hear now: "How can we be taken more seriously as a profession? How do we prove we're not just creative people who don't understand the business? How do we get a seat at the top table?"

But I think the marketing profession is a little ahead in its mission to get closer to the seat of power. My guess is that there are more marketing directors out there than internal communication directors. But whether that's because they do truly understand the business better, or because many leaders still rate external branding and communication over internal engagement, is debatable.

IB: So what, in your opinion, are the biggest challenges internal communicators now face?

MT: In Melcrum's recent survey of internal communication trends, as many as 50 percent of communicators said they weren't able to prove the ROI of internal communication and so it's not surprising that measuring their effectiveness and securing the appropriate level of budget for their functions is still a big priority.

Other challenges include:

- motivating employees to align to the business strategy
- helping employees to cope with information overload
- harnessing new technology
- communicating to diverse audiences
- improving leadership and management communication.

Not surprisingly, the top five areas for increased investment over the coming year are predicted to be:

- the intranet
- communication training for senior leaders
- communication training for managers
- measurement
- new technology.

IB: Despite the overwhelming evidence to suggest that face-to-face communication is the most effective, it will be interesting to see what proportion of future budgetary spend goes on the intranet and new technology instead.

MT: Again, balance is key. On an organizational level, I think the biggest challenges internal communicators face are:

- *Strategy* – do employees know the business strategy and understand what's expected from them?
- *Engagement* – do employees feel enough of a connection to the business to deliver the strategy?
- *Continuous change* – how do you maintain productivity and focus in the face of constant change and reaction to external market conditions?

On a professional level, in my view, the biggest challenges internal communicators face are:

- demonstrating a real understanding of business

- earning the opportunity to work more closely with senior leaders
- developing skills associated with more strategic communication, like communication coaching, root cause analysis and managing change.

Mandy's observations, although informed by her interactions with a lot of people within the industry, aren't just anecdotal but are backed up by research conducted regularly by Melcrum. I believe that Mandy's answers to the last two questions are particularly revealing in the context of this book.

Many people are still attracted to the profession by a fondness for the tactical aspects of the job, contributing toward and running a newsroom, crafting and distributing messages in the hope of spreading good news, working with agencies to develop funky new tools and so on, and, on the face of it, not really confronting as much direct risk as their externally focused colleagues. Take this current job advertisement in the national press as an example.

A leading global financial services provider is looking for a head of internal communications to join one of its project teams, providing expert advice and guidance on all matters relating to distribution, publishing and input to the development of new channels.

I would compare this perspective of the internal communication market to the oft-aired HR cliché of "I joined the profession to help people," when, as we know, the realities of managing change are often more involved with the dark arts of downsizing, handling difficult messages, and dealing with tricky interpersonal issues than they are to do with benevolence.

The best internal communicators recognize that the role is far from disembodied, tactical, without risk or, indeed, easy. Compared to their external-facing colleagues, internal communicators have to convince audiences made up of their peers and colleagues; people who know a brand promise from a lie and who can't be fooled or charmed for long by gloss, glitz, gimmicks, and fancy external branding, particularly when their colleagues or projects may have been impacted by cost controls.

Employees and customers are looking through the same brand

window but through very different lenses (Figure 3.3). Employees don't have the same brand expectations of the corporate brand internally as they do externally with the brand as a consumer. They expect less razzmatazz and greater sincerity. They are closer to the means of production and the delivery mechanisms that drive the service and are fully aware of any breaches in the service chain, irrespective of the brand promise. Because they're in this position, employees are the first to notice any disconnection between the espoused externalized brand and the actual, and if this disconnection is down to anything other than the ebb and flow of natural tolerances and verges on overpromising or insincerity, it impacts their ability to deliver at the front line as well as how they behave as customers. Whether they're forgiving or not depends upon the degree to which they believe in the leadership and are engaged with the mission of the business.

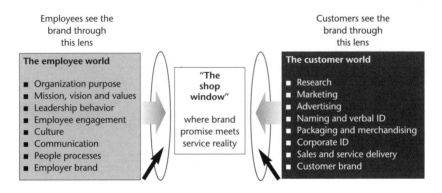

FIGURE 3.3 **The brand window**

The current Nationwide Building Society advertisements in the UK effectively lampoon this relationship, with the comical junior manager giving humorous satirical voice to the murky reality of the bogus financial service brand; a world which most customers suspect exists, but don't always see. Insincerity has worryingly become such a norm within this sector that organizations are now satirizing themselves hoping the consumer will think "at least this lot are aware of the shortcomings of their sector, so perhaps they'll be more honest with customers like me."

To a certain extent, consumers are buying dreams and are willing to put up with a slight disconnection between the brand and reality if the brand allows them the luxury of fantasy; as long as the gap between fantasy and reality isn't too extreme. Was it Somerset Maughan who said: "what do we have but our illusions – what do we ask of others but we be allowed to keep them?"?

Employees, on the other hand, don't always have the luxury of fantasy when they live and breathe the brand. They can choose to reside in blissful ignorance for a time, but again, it depends on the degree to which their motivators are being addressed by the organization. They will usually tolerate short-term suspensions of higher order benefits in pursuit of the promised land of a vision of the future. But threaten their basic needs and you do so at your peril.

EMPLOYMENT BRAND

A relatively recent phenomenon has been the creation of a concept of inward-facing brand management under the umbrella term, "employment brand." The term is meant to represent the manifestation of the organization's brand through the core people processes like recruitment, induction, and performance management. It's a drive that has arisen as a by-product of the application of marketing methodology to the internal market. It has succeeded in raising the profile of internal communication. But internal communication isn't internal marketing.

What has emerged has been a tug-of-war between marketing and HR over the internal depiction of the brand and brand values in particular. In fact, some organizations, quite unnecessarily in my view, have given license to a virtual values industry, where a distinct set of values and behaviors have been created for the internal market, owned by HR, while the external brand values are owned by marketing (Figure 3.4). It hasn't helped to drive clarity or engagement.

Whether the values have been distilled or not, the employment brand equation is a relatively simple one for me – it is the espoused brand, "how we're supposed to do things round here" (the employer brand, if you will) minus the actual employee experience "how we actually do things round here."

Potential employees are juggling a range of motives when making employment decisions, of which brand and projected values is one. Why should the brand projected by the recruiters differ fundamentally from the externalized brand?

The act of creating a distinct brand for the internal market is just another version of brand creep; it's confusing and ultimately counterproductive. Yes, ensure that the brand espoused internally matches the brand delivered but start with the existing brand characteristics and values and involve marketing. The effort to create this industry as an add-on to organizational development would be better spent trying to forge partnerships between the internal and external-facing communicators in pursuit of a holistic form of brand engagement.

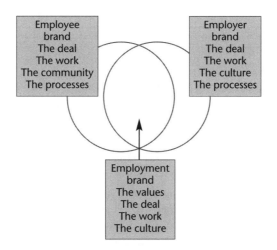

FIGURE 3.4 **Employment brand model**

Not connecting?

One of the difficulties communicators face is the proliferation of push-focused communication tactics gleaned from the strategy of client communication, including tactics like the use of direct mail. Consider this quote from Professor Phillip Kitchen:

> Direct mail is the third fastest growing area of marketing communication, behind interactive marketing and brand PR/sponsorship. DM generated 20 per cent of all UK marcom expenditure in 2004, significantly ahead of the European norm (compared to 40 per cent for advertising, 16 per cent for PR/sponsorship, 16 per cent for sales promotion, and 8 per cent for interactive). (quoted in Buckingham, 2007)

As we know, however, growth in spending doesn't always equate to the achievement of objectives and, as Professor Kitchen points out:

There is a widespread and recognisable trend that:

a) much of direct mail material is directed toward the nearest round file that comes to hand

b) consumers and customers are fast growing intolerant toward 'nuisance communications'. (quoted in Buckingham, 2007)

When direct mail only achieves an estimated 2 percent success rate in the external market, what exactly is the point of this type of push communication in the internal market other than to tick the box on the project update sheet marked "communicated"?

Time and time again I've seen examples of project managers who believe their project to be the single most important initiative on the corporate horizon, pushing missives into the stream of corporate consciousness only to find that their target response rates have washed up on the shores of indifference. Even when the subject matter has a massive "there's loads in this for you" factor, poorly positioned and badly crafted communication that isn't involving will get lost, get filed or get ignored. I've seen benefits updates, pensions reviews and share scheme launches, subjects which should at least make the internal audience sit up and listen, fail miserably due to programmatic push communication and an absence of involvement in the design of the communication. Yet the campaigns were seen as successful in terms of campaign design, timeline adherence and project management. Some even won awards. Too often the communication department takes scant responsibility for the achievement of the goals of the function promoting the scheme

A common fallback when faced with communication difficulties is for both parties to point fingers and create an "us and them" mentality, usually as a survival strategy (we naturally fear what we don't understand). "Why do I keep getting these booklets and who do they think they are telling me that I should be lucky to work here? Do they take me for an idiot? They should have saved the money they spent on the fancy copywriting." "I don't know why we bother to update staff on the pension scheme, as half of them are too thick to understand." This establishment/antiestablishment impulse is more pronounced within the hothouse of organizational

culture and can make the task of the internal communicator ener-
vating at times.

Authenticity, sincerity, clarity, credibility, and, most important,
involvement are the internal communicator's allies in getting employees
on board. But it is far from an easy task, especially if there is confusion
about the corporate culture and value set in which they're operating, or
if they're being subtly asked by the leaders to deal in half-truths.

Despite the increasing challenge and growing importance of the
role, however, opportunities to influence upstream activity via places
at the top table have to be earned. This calls for a credible understanding of business basics, strategic nous, a resolute focus on financial
results, and tough but effective interpersonal skills.

Until we start to see internal communicators' résumés heralding a
legacy of frontline business experience blended with a history of relevant skills development, it's extremely difficult to envisage a ladder of
upward progression leading from newsroom to boardroom. But if the
marketing profession has had to develop the skills to justify a place,
it's a journey their internal communication counterparts can take,
provided they can find a way to prove the impact of their efforts,
make the transition from tactical to strategic, have an appetite for
partnership, and can come out of the shadow of HR and marketing.
There are, of course, some notable exceptions, but they're rarely
found networking at conferences. This is what Mandy Thatcher had
to say on the subject:

> There's plenty of good news about. There's growing confidence
> among some practitioners who are starting to receive the recog-
> nition they deserve – and are reaping the rewards. However, the
> profession is still seeking to gain more respect internally and focus
> on its own professional development. The fact that 38 percent of
> respondents reported an increase or a dramatic increase in their
> budgets in the last 12 months seems to bear out that organizations
> are recognizing the importance of internal communication and
> valuing the practitioners in those roles. In 2004, for example, that
> figure was around 10 percent lower.

As we know, money talks. The challenge is to find more effective
ways to demonstrate to the business the return on that investment
(see Figures 3.5–3.8).

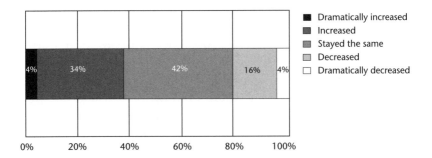

FIGURE 3.5 **How internal communication budgets (including salaries) have changed in the past 12 months**

Source: The Pulse © Melcrum Publishing, 2006

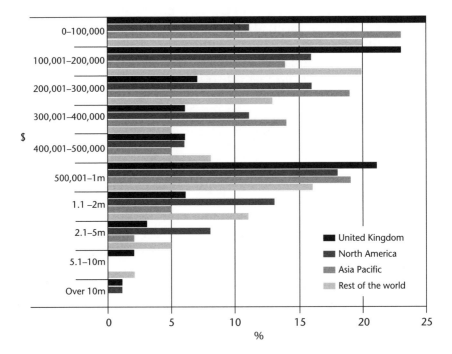

FIGURE 3.6 **Total internal communication budget by region**

Source: The Pulse © Melcrum Publishing, 2006

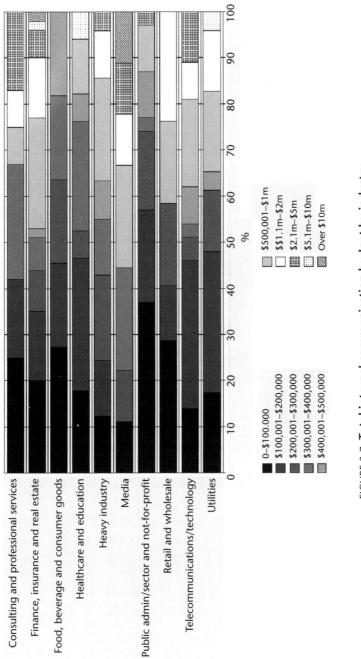

FIGURE 3.7 **Total internal communication budget by industry**

Source: The Pulse © Melcrum Publishing, 2006

Legend:
- 0–$100.000
- $100,001–$200,000
- $200,001–$300,000
- $300,001–$400,000
- $400,001–$500,000
- $500,001–$1m
- $$1.1m–$2m
- $2.1m–$5m
- $5.1m–$10m
- Over $10m

Industries:
- Consulting and professional services
- Finance, insurance and real estate
- Food, beverage and consumer goods
- Healthcare and education
- Heavy industry
- Media
- Public admin/sector and not-for-profit
- Retail and wholesale
- Telecommunications/technology
- Utilities

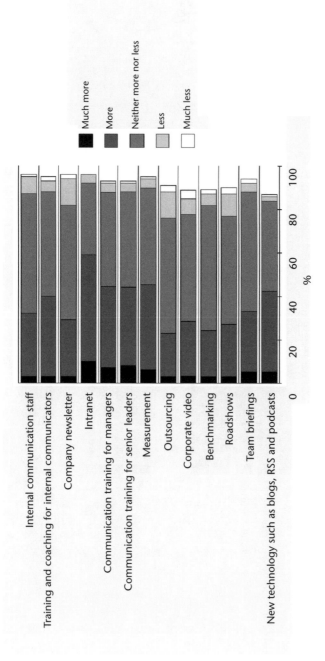

Much more

More

Neither more nor less

Less

Much less

FIGURE 3.8 **How budget allocation is predicted to change over the next 12 months**

Source: The Pulse © Melcrum Publishing, 2006

ENGAGE PEOPLE BY LETTING THEM PLAY

The interview with Mandy helps to highlight the development journey that the internal communication profession is on. Figure 3.9, which I co-developed a number of years ago now and which has stood the test of time, provides a visual representation of the communication continuum. It clearly shows the best possible outcome achievable in response to a range of communication techniques.

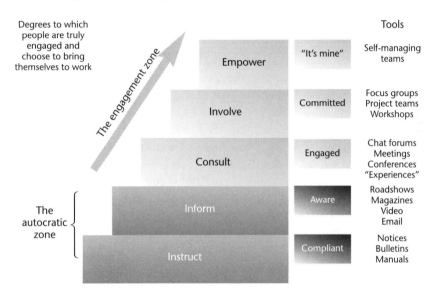

FIGURE 3.9 **The engagement staircase**

While each element of the communication mix has its place in the internal communicator's toolbox, true engagement comes from providing stakeholders with opportunities to interact with and explore the content via the media. The key is to have a broad range of expertise and to be flexible.

Push communication based around instruction and compliance has its place, but how many examples can you think of where blind compliance is the required outcome? Even health and safety communication is arguably better achieved by aiming for true engagement rather than brainless compliance. This point was illustrated perfectly at a recent seminar when a junior officer from the army stood up and asked how he could ensure that his communiqués were taken seriously, as some of his missives were issued on what he called "an extreme need to know basis." He had just designed an electronic newsletter and was increasingly frustrated that soldiers weren't reading it, despite being instructed to do so. Yet an unofficial, satirical, cartoon-based rag, produced by the "squaddies," could be found everywhere on camp. They were also experiencing a graffiti campaign in the public latrines. Anyone care to put two and two together for him?

We'll return to the notion of guerrilla communication and the engagement continuum in greater detail later on, but it's worth making the point here in the context of how existing internal communication professionals are prioritizing their time and resources.

Pumping messages into the market, however well crafted, simply isn't enough, once we appreciate that brands are living, organic, social organisms. They are the sum of behaviors that manifest values, represented through design, but which need to be experienced if they're to be fully understood. You can't teach about a culture and expect pupils to know what the food tastes like, what it feels like to wear the clothes, buy the product, or sit through a creative meeting. They have to live it, explore it, feel it, have a chance to interact and play with it and then to volunteer ideas and suggestions based upon their experiences and this, for me, is the essence of employee brand engagement.

INSIDE-OUT COMMUNICATION (THE POWER OF PARTNERSHIP)

In conversation with two tier one communicators

Caroline Hempstead (VP group corporate communication) and Wendy Russell (head of R&D corporate affairs) are representatives of the tier one professional communication cadre. They are both currently based in the UK but between them have many years' international experience including the US, Asia, and Continental Europe. Ironically, their metaphoric paths crossed recently when Wendy left pharmaceutical giant AstraZeneca where she had worked her way from sales, line management, and training and development roles into medical and product communications initially and then corporate communications. She joined the UK Department of Health shortly before Caroline joined AZ, having had a long and successful career at Shell. Caroline started her professional communications career in the PR department of iconic English retail and lifestyle brand Harrods.

Having known and worked with them both for the last six years or so, I recently caught up with them to gather their perspectives on the changes they've witnessed within the communications field and market.

IB: How have you seen the profession develop over the past 10 years?

CH: For me, the biggest change has been the fact that the profession now takes itself more seriously and is taken much more seriously. In pursuit of a competitive edge or to respond to shareholder pressure, businesses have to be far more fleet of foot, to reinvent themselves frequently, change is a constant and communication is vital to mobilize people. Importantly, the change has to start at the top.

WR: It has definitely become more professional. Over the past decade, we have seen more communications and corporate affairs specialists sitting at the top table in businesses and organizations, and a growing number of chief executives who have come from this background.

IB: What have been the biggest developments in channel management?

WR: Ten years ago, the internet was just starting to become a serious form of business communication (we often forget that it's such a fresh phenomenon). I had the opportunity to develop the first internet site for Zeneca Pharmaceuticals at about this time. Electronic communication was also kicking off. Before, we communicated with external sites and overseas markets via fax and telex. Now there is a real richness in the channels for communication, allowing more targeted messages, if used properly.

IB: "Used properly" is absolutely right. Looking across sectors, there's been an explosion in electronic communication. Social media is rife in the external brand market, which is challenging traditional notions of control. We've seen a deal of demand for internal tools to deal with the frightening rise in "message traffic," when the real answer often lies in more effective and judicious use of channels employing classic engagement best practices.

CH: Interestingly, advances in media are helping to drive up people's expectations as well as liberate their ability to communicate irrespective of formal channels. As people grow accustomed to new media (podcasts, blogs, webcasts, and social networking sites such as Facebook and so on) as an integral part of their home lives, they expect to see these in the workplace. The days of the internal communication cascade aren't numbered but they are only one piece in the puzzle now, when they used to dominate.

IB: In your role, what's the importance of brand?

CH: The corporate brand plays a critical role in embodying the vision and values of the company, it's the constant, the seat of stability and vital as the expression of the vision, the long game, especially during times of insecurity and change. People demand to refer back to the corporate brand as the repository of the story, the point of reference providing the compass for the direction of the business. For example, at AZ, when we post a message on the intranet from the CEO, who is seen as the owner of the vision, we get the same number of hits as there are staff, within a week. But there's little doubt that, day to day, it is the product or team brands that people are most wedded to, which gives a clue to the importance of middle managers as communicators.

IB: I know it's a perspective you can share, Wendy, having worked on both product and corporate communication, but I'm particularly interested in the relevance of brand now that you've crossed over to the public sector. I recently met one of the directors of a consultancy specializing in the public sector. Oddly, he claims that brands have little relevance in his sector, when it's my experience that much of the criticism the sector has attracted is down to a reactionary attitude to change, which is a reflection of the culture, values, and self-perception of the people who work there – many of the key behavioral components of internal brand.

WR: Your contact can't be more wrong, I'm afraid. The National Institute for Health Research (NIHR), established as a virtual organization in April 2006, provides a key mechanism through which the Department of Health will deliver the new R&D strategy set out in *Best Research for Best Health*. It has been very important to us to establish a strong brand, linked to the NHS brand, for the NIHR. The reason for the link with the NHS rather than Department of Health is that the health research that NIHR commissions and the people who conduct the research are within the NHS. Also, many of the programs that are funded by the NIHR have, over the years, developed identities of their own. A major program that we are currently implementing is to synchronize these with the NIHR corporate brand. Brand management is going to be a key component of the communications mix within this sector in the future, where joined-up thinking is very much needed.

IB: You both deal with a wide range of stakeholders. How do you divide your time between the internal and external aspects of your role?

CH: I currently split my time about 50/50 between internal and external communications. Because of the major change program at Shell, my time was weighted toward the internal market.

The tools we use aren't that different for the respective stakeholders: voice, print, electronic, broadcast, and so on, although one of the biggest challenges is to recognize that different stakeholder groups have different perspectives on company news. For example, an announcement about a strategic divestment in line with business strategy will be perceived positively by external stakeholders but is much harder for the internal market to swallow. In these instances, the role of the line manager is critical in interpreting and contextualizing the message for employees.

WR: My role is currently more balanced toward external communication, as much of the business is done through contracted third parties and so there is a strong element of communication that is focused on these key partners. Again, similar principles apply though.

IB: Having recently crossed over, Wendy, how would you characterize the difference between your private sector past and public sector present?

WR: Rather than looking for difference, I would say that there are many similarities in my experience. Where I work, within the Research and Development Directorate at the Department of Health, we are goal-oriented and future-focused, with a determination to make a difference to the health and wealth of the nation. It's at the core of our brand, you might say. Delivery and indeed quality of delivery are very important.

IB: So your job is to help connect employees, stakeholders, and ultimately customers with this vision and the core values that underpin the DoH.

WR: Absolutely. In the pharmaceutical industry, or private sector, much of this also applies but is given a commercial bias. The workforce generally has a high level of intelligence and integrity. In the cancer area, which accounted for a fair proportion of the R&D at Alderley Park in the northwest, employees felt really passionate about the prospect of bringing products to the market that would improve outcomes for patients with this disease, for example Arimidex (anastrozole) for breast cancer. It's fair to say that this was ultimately more motivating to most than the commercial demands of the business and worked best when they both went hand in hand. Working for a brand that makes this sort of difference really helps.

IB: It would appear that communicators in both sectors would do well to blend brand engagement thinking and pragmatic benevolence, or a focus on core values. With this thought in mind, what critical success factors would you highlight when managing internal communications?

WR: Three things spring to mind:

1. Improving the performance and delivery of the organization

2. Getting the best value from the resources employed

3. Ensuring everyone understands their role in delivering the organization's strategy and feels ownership.

CH: I would add:

- having a clear, integrated communication plan, with clearly identified outcomes for all stakeholder groups (internal and external)

- having good quality, two-way communication channels

- prioritizing key messages and managing links between the audience segments.

IB: You've both obviously known a few communicators within the businesses you've worked for and within the industry, but what would you say are the characteristics of a highly effective communicator?

CH: Reflecting back on the best role models and most effective communicators I've known, they are all:

- astute business leaders who are positive about engagement, not just pushing information

- good at simplifying and staying on message, linking information to develop a consistent story, adapted for audiences
- comfortable in their own skin, so their communication is authentic and consistent with other aspects of their leadership style. They are as good at listening as they are communicating. Because they're being themselves, they're inspirational but also predictable, which adds to the credibility of the message.

WR: I very much agree with Caroline's observations and would reiterate that, for me, the most important trait is focus on facilitating the delivery of bottom line benefits.

Elizabeth Sozanski, the first VP of internal communications in AstraZeneca, springs to mind. She was appointed shortly after the merger. She is passionate, determined, not afraid to challenge accepted practices, creative, and (possibly more than she ought to be) willing to take on the detail of delivery.

In my view, top communication professionals need to possess excellent business skills if they're to be taken seriously and have strategic vision, but not be above getting their hands dirty. Interestingly, Elizabeth is now a senior director of marketing strategy with the company, a role where the link to results is very explicit.

IB: We've established that communication is key to delivering against business objectives, which includes leveraging the brand. Taking a look at this diagram of what the BY2W team believe are the issues keeping internal communicators awake at night (Figure 3.10), what do you see as the biggest challenges communicators face now?

CH: Getting and maintaining a place at the top table. Credible communicators nearly always have to be able to punch above their weight, attracting and retaining real quality talent with the right mix of strategic as well as tactical qualities (despite the common myth that anyone can communicate, not everyone is suited to the role). Ensuring partnerships between the essential disciplines, for example legal, investor relations and finance on the external side, HR, employee relations and organization development on the internal side (it's not as easy as it sounds, especially in a downsizing or change scenario).

WR: It seems to me that communicators exist in two worlds at present, with a large underbelly of the profession viewed as message deliverers. Yet, if we aren't careful, we'll all continue to be "tarred with the same brush." That must change if the role is

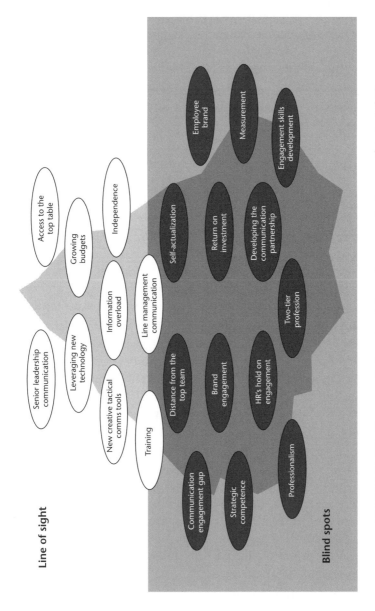

Line of sight

Access to the top table

Senior leadership communication

Growing budgets

Independence

Leveraging new technology

Information overload

Line management communication

New creative tactical comms tools

Training

Employee brand

Measurement

Engagement skills development

Self-actualization

Return on investment

Developing the communication partnership

Two-tier profession

Distance from the top team

Brand engagement

HR's hold on engagement

Communication engagement gap

Strategic competence

Professionalism

Blind spots

FIGURE 3.10 **What's currently keeping internal communicators awake at night?**

to gain critical mass and continue to evolve. It is not just a challenge for the communication specialist but also for the executive teams who are not always aware what professional communication can achieve. I see internal communication as the glue between the key communication functions. It needs to be hand in glove with both HR and marketing, yet marketing and HR tend to have a much more distant relationship, except on the transactional side.

The greatest challenge is maintaining the momentum behind the development of the profession and embedding the "new" role for professional communicators in contributing to improved business performance and brand reputation, regardless of sector.

BEHAVIORAL BRAND CREEP

Reams have been dedicated to the creation of the physical assets that represent the most obvious, tangible manifestations of brand. In my experience, this is where most of the brand management time, energy, and expense are invested. Odd, when it's the intangibles, the behavioral factors that invariably matter the most. Yet this aspect seldom features in the marketing or HR budget.

Most of us have heard of the notion of "brand creep." It's a term usually applied to the subtle mutation of a brand as a result of small changes made over time and is normally a negative term, as it implies that the physical parameters of the brand have changed, to the extent that the brand no longer represents its founding purpose. The brand has become distorted, misshapen.

Gargantuan brands like McDonald's, Coca-Cola, and BP employ large teams of brand managers who act as enforcers, scouring the planet to ensure that not only do outsiders refrain from compromising their brand, but the invaluable brand guidelines are fully complied with by their associates and stakeholders. This sort of brand policing signals how precious the mega-brands are about their brand equity, and for good reason.

I once participated in a global meeting called by the marketing executives of a well-known Asian car manufacturer, who insisted that all their national brand managers attended, along with their brand agencies and suppliers. A frenzy of square glasses, sharp suits, and sharper hairstyles was promised.

For once, someone had taken it upon himself to join up the dots as part of a program of aggressively repositioning the precious brand. Customer feedback suggested that the market had become confused about the positioning of the brand relative to their key competitors and this was seriously impacting both costs and sales.

After a period of investigation, he discovered that the agencies and country managers had been subtly interpreting the central brand guidelines in their own way for some time, and through applying unique layers of expensive but poorly focused regional creativity down the years, brand creep had become an epidemic. The important connection with the core brand had been gradually undermined.

With a single gathering, however, he was able to address the issue, and start the process of bringing everyone back onto the same design page. He realigned them (not a dirty word in process management circles). He also rationalized huge swathes of agency spend, refocused supplier-related processes, and vowed to invest in what he called "brand training" for employees and partners. I can still hear the massed protestations about stifled comparative creativity. Call it a coincidence but the brand in question has not only stopped the financial rot but has come on in leaps and bounds since then.

This is an extreme example of how brand creep can have a substantial impact on the bottom line as well as the power of shared thinking. Oddly, however, the notion of brand creep isn't really applied to the behavioral aspects of the brand, possibly because there isn't always a budget for it, possibly because it's harder to prove or possibly, despite the efforts of the agencies to create a lucrative new market, behavior simply can't be aligned in quite the same "process and rule"-driven way. In short, it's tough to manage.

Again, the likes of the mega-process managers, including McDonald's, take a legendary interest in ensuring consistency of training and delivery, but in more complex service industries, how much thought and effort actually goes into ensuring that:

- key people processes are in line with and reinforce the brand?
- values and behaviors are consistent with and reinforce the brand?

Interestingly, in the example I've just given, no mechanisms were in place at the time to assess employee feedback. But they were included in the customer focus groups.

It's a core belief of mine that, without structure, innovation and initiative are simply chaotic and ultimately self-defeating. Creativity is the spark that lights the fires of innovation but, without focus, it can rage uncontrollably.

Take as an example the recent scandal regarding phone-in competition lines, particularly affecting the British media companies including the British Broadcasting Corporation, the iconic, BBC brand. For decades, it has made a business out of being perceived as an ambassador for many of the finer values associated with Englishness, including fairness, impartiality, integrity, autonomy (despite the BBC's funding base), and trust. It has prided itself as being a purveyor of cultured broadcasting and a number of director generals have even been criticized for seemingly adopting the position of de facto moral arbiter in the national culture debate.

Needless to say, it is the ultimate ignominy for this brand to be associated with incidents that have included falsifying and misrepresenting competition winners, and for these incidents to have happened during some of the BBC's flagship shows, a number involving charity fundraising and shows directed at children. The BBC clearly survives but we've recently witnessed a brand disaster of major proportions that will have lasting repercussions. This is an incident where the corporation and national brand arguably are both tainted.

To make matters worse, the incidents don't appear to have been simple one-off mistakes. There appear to have been a series of seemingly deliberate, extremely misguided deceptions, which at best implies that a select number of relatively powerful staff are not sufficiently in tune with all the key values of the BBC. Perhaps even more worrying is the implication that the formal BBC brand values may have gradually eroded until they may well be out of tune with the current BBC culture. However you look at it, brand creep has had a significant negative impact on the brand.

Whether this alleged situation has developed as a result of competition within the market or a breakdown of the BBC's core people processes, only time will tell, but it is clear that these incidents are examples of behavioral brand creep leading rapidly to brand disaster and the consequences are far-reaching. The same mistakes made by a number of their independent broadcasting colleagues cost millions but for the BBC, the immediate impact on its brand has arguably been greater given the unique status of its brand among broadcasters. Doubtless the BBC will survive but as BBC supremo Mark Thompson has made clear, it will certainly have to change. Part of that change should be a thorough investigation of the state the internal culture and values platform from which they, as well as ITV and, some would suggest, the entire pantheon of broadcasting, are operating as a way of revolutionizing internal brand engagement across the industry.

BRANDSCAPE AND THE BRAND ENGAGEMENT JOURNEY

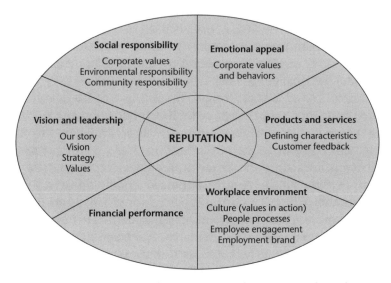

FIGURE 3.11 **Typical components of a corporate brand**

There are conflicting opinions about the core ingredients that go into the brand recipe, but focusing on the simple oval matrix, shown in Figure 3.11, illustrates that apparent intangibles like behaviors, values, and interpersonal aspects constitute the lion's share of brand equity.

Interbrand has made an international name for itself predominantly on the back of its highly sophisticated, innovative, and much respected brand valuation metrics and international brand ranking process and has achieved worldwide recognition for its annual survey *The 100 Top Brands*.

Among the ingredients Interbrand takes into account when developing its annual poll is understanding the percentage of a company's revenues that can be credited to a brand. To qualify for the list, each brand must have publicly available marketing and financial data and generate about a third of its earnings outside its own country. The brand must also be recognizable outside its customer base.

It then deducts operating costs, taxes, and a charge for the capital employed to arrive at the intangible earnings. The calculation strips out intangibles such as patents and management strength to assess what portion of those earnings can be attributed to the brand. Finally the brand's strength is assessed to determine the risk profile of those earnings forecasts. Considerations include market leadership, stability, and global reach – or the ability to cross both geographic and cultural borders. That generates a discount rate, which is applied to brand earnings to get a net present value.

I used to be an Interbrand director and am aware that Interbrand's methodology is an example of the type of metrics that have contributed greatly to the credibility of brand management in the boardroom, where brand equity should most certainly be a balance sheet consideration of as much interest to the CEO and FD as the marketing director. It's a language that certainly helps to captivate, engage, and focus the top team and is increasingly being taken into account in M&A due diligence analysis.

Brand valuation is an important part of the brand equation, as it renders the previously intangible into a calculable asset, whatever valuation formula you may favor. But once you've arrived at a net present value (NPV), it obviously isn't enough to then simply focus on the tangible assets like:

- naming and verbal identity
- corporate identity
- design assets
- packaging and even digital branding.

It's easier and comparatively simple to cost, but when you compare it to the matrix in Figure 3.11, it still falls short as it can't take into account the value of intangibles like the fitness for purpose of organization culture. If most of the brand value actually rests in the intangibles – the culture, loyalty, values, and behaviors of employees when interacting with each other and with your customers – you should certainly be doing a lot to understand the health of your people processes and to keep people engaged if you're to retain their loyalty and focus. Acquisitive organizations like ARM or the canny venture capitalist will look to the intangible brand assets when making future assessments and the enlightened CEO will be looking for ways to assess and then leverage this behavioral capital now, in order to stay several steps ahead.

MERGERS AND ACQUISITIONS

When two major pharmaceutical companies merged to form AstraZeneca, those enlightened pharma brains had worked out that not only did the brand merger deal make sense on the balance sheet, but the merger of a brand defined by a predominantly innovative culture with a more rational and focused one was a winning combination. The new board placed great stock in understanding the complementary cultures and working on the communication vehicles to make the most of the opportunities presented by the cultures coming together.

The same reflections came to mind when the RWE and npower deal was brokered, which is why the externalized npower brand has remained relatively unchanged in its physical and behavioral manifestations and the employment brand has actually been strengthened by the structure change, despite npower being the junior partner. In fact, it is so emboldened that npower has now positioned itself confidently as a challenger brand in spite of the tricky period the energy market is going through.

When the low-key Mexican brand CEMEX, worldwide producer of cement, ready-mix concrete and aggregates, made a swift and unexpected acquisition of UK establishment brand RMC, however, UK managers and staff were taken by surprise and feared the worst. I know; I was running workshops with some of its board around this time, and they were just awakening to the compelling need for change.

Yet CEMEX has become extremely adept at learning from each acquisition, is proficient at managing the internal communication associated with its acquisitiveness, works hard and fast to maintain a "business as usual" mentality, and quickly proves added value in aspects of the business in which it arguably leads the world, namely process reengineering and improvement. Like ARM, it has become practiced in understating its own culture and reiterating what it respects about the organization and brand it has just acquired, yet insists on clear performance goals and targets. A case of clear objectives and positive strokes combined with quick wins, which not only helps to restore confidence, alleviate fear, and build self-respect but also makes employees' lives easier – a core motivator. CEMEX understands the power of brand engagement, delivers early results, and emphasizes the best qualities of the merging cultures. It's certainly worked at RMC, where feedback has been extremely positive, especially from hitherto seldom heard outposts of the RMC organization.

When undertaking a brand development program, whether as part of a major structure change or not, the answer isn't to define the brand, identify the assets, and then conscript and align the business with them. It doesn't work with customers, so why should it work with employees, despite the fact that they're on the payroll? The answer's to build from the ground up.

Technology has liberated guerrilla communication to the point that brand managers really struggle to contain and own communication about their brand, whether sanctioned or otherwise. Even brand ambassadors can verge on the worryingly fanatical. Type virtually any iconic brand into a search engine, MySpace or YouTube and you'll eventually discover unsanctioned commentary and content in the form of either a homage by passionate fanatics buzzing around the brand like a hive of bees round corporate honey, or a highly critical alter-brand ego, like that created recently by eco-warriors who've targeted SUVs like the Tahoe by Chevrolet or the self-styled "spiritual warriors" who, following an internet campaign playfully objecting to stuffy institutionalism, ensured that over 390,000 people registered as Jedi knights in the 2001 census of faiths or belief systems undertaken by the UK's Office of National Statistics. Brands and icons are being set loose from their brand guideline straitjackets whether their originators and custodians like it or not. The same is happening in the internal market where employees will find a way round overly dictatorial cascade communication.

"Control is out of control ... the notion of control is over. Your brand has to be out in the open," says Jackie Huba, a business adviser and co-author (with Ben McConnell) of *Citizen Marketers: When People Are the Message* (2006).

This time of brand terrorism is certainly worrying for vulnerable brand managers exposed by the ineffectiveness of censorship or corporate governance. But is it really a problem if the message your brand is sending out is in tune with its social context? Starting to think about brand values differently now? Isn't it about time that notions like corporate social responsibility are reappraised and brought to the fore as engagement drivers?

But it shouldn't take a catalyst like fear of sabotage to recognize that employee engagement does involve letting go a little. As we've explored, involvement, making a contribution is what drives interest and ultimately ownership. Brand managers need to learn to take a few risks and encourage the latent creativity in everyone rather than hogging the creative bit and expecting their peers to comply with the dry guidelines. Why spend all that time searching the wide open blue skies for the bird of inspiration, enthusiasm, and differentiation, only to stick it in a gilded cage at the first opportunity and teach it to sing a tune you can barely whistle?

But how do you ensure that customers and employees are delivering a money-making service and how do you go about developing a joined-up approach to brand management that includes both behavioral and material aspects?

THE QUEST FOR BALANCE

In their book *Brand Manners*, Pringle and Gordon (2001) set out four different dimensions, which they say define a customer experience and which, in turn, define a brand:

1. The rational experience – what goes on
2. The emotional experience – how we feel
3. The political experience – why it is right for us
4. The spiritual experience – where it leads us to or "whither."

Applying their four dimensions gives a balanced business perspective to brand thinking. Mindful of this notion of balanced thinking, I advocate a simple engagement process.

If we accept that a brand is the sum of the material and behavioral manifestations of the promises made to staff and customers, achieving a successful outcome in any holistic brand engagement exercise is then reliant upon:

- negotiating a coalition between the brand stakeholders (traditionally marketing, communication, HR and the office of the chief executive)
- having a clear and simple process
- role modeling the brand values during the process

■ developing a hard-nosed business case for undertaking the exercise in the first place.

Figure 3.12 shows the four stages of the brand engagement journey, which I will now expand upon in more detail.

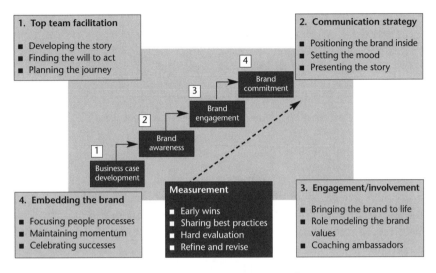

FIGURE 3.12 **The "brand engagement" journey**

Business case development

The metrics contributing toward the calculation of brand NPV vary. But they clearly need to include hard facts relating to the key performance indicators (KPIs) of the business. And they need to be balanced.

Interbrand's brand valuation model is a good starting place. We then need to factor in other critical customer, employee, and process management measures that are important to the goals of the business and the achievement of the vision. Balanced scorecard thinking should do the trick.

Too often in the past, the hard, brand-related facts have been owned and managed exclusively by the marketing function, the rational promise makers, without a bridging partnership with the spiritual, political and emotional custodians of the brand, the promise keepers (traditionally HR but increasingly a coalition involving the director of organization development and director of internal communication/

employee engagement in their own right). Data relating to both customer and employee worlds are critical and need to be considered in unison, as both sides of the looking glass need to be factored into the equation.

It's during these initial steps that the battle for effective brand management is often won or lost:

1. If the representation of the business case isn't sufficiently inclusive of the board as a whole
2. If the critical parties aren't represented at the top table
3. If the goals aren't balanced and representative.

Get this step wrong and the coalition will fail as:

1. They aren't all accountable
2. They aren't all involved.

While it is clearly vital to make the business case for effective brand management at board level, in practice, it will fall to the real ceos, the chief engagement officers, throughout the business to translate and make the business case for the promise keepers, the frontline staff. And that calls for a different language and an approach based on goals and objectives, reflected in their performance management contracts. Only line managers can do this effectively. Again, fail to develop an inclusive business case and a balanced portfolio of goals at the start and the brand remains "someone else's problem."

Brand awareness

It is in these partnership discussions where the role modeling comes in and usually where external facilitation is most useful for:

- gathering qualitative and quantitative data objectively
- providing benchmarking data
- owning and facilitating the core process
- encouraging blue-sky as well as grounded thinking
- enabling a values-based leadership approach
- stimulating the creation of the story
- suggesting types of goals and targets.

I sometimes refer to this stage as a brandscape analysis and it breaks down into two parts:

- *Understanding the current brand position* – where are we now, what does it look and feel like, how are we performing against all KPIs?
- *Agreeing the desired future position* – articulation of who we want to be, what that looks and feels like, how we'll make it happen (the engagement process), and how we'll measure progress.

Starting with the rational perspective and then warming up to explore the emotional, political, and (if they're brave and comfortable in their own skins), spiritual dimensions of the brand is possible with sensitive team and individual coaching. I talk later on about techniques for achieving this transition but suffice to say that, at this stage, in order to bring structure, focus, and a degree of process to the behavior discussion, some form of framework helps a great deal. Figure 3.13 shows the outline of the behavioral brand framework.

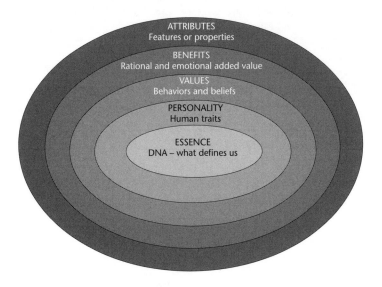

FIGURE 3.13 **The behavioral brand framework**

The framework in action is illustrated in Figure 3.14 by overlaying an example of the analysis we undertook for a clinical research organization.

In this case, in order to be a fully engaging process, we undertook the brandscape analysis as part of a comprehensive workshop with the top team, at which we explored the company's market, challenges, hopes and fears, vision for the business, role modeling of values, and perceived versus required culture. There isn't an exclusive top-down requirement and, in this case, the consultation process involved a large sample of stakeholders, but it was sorely needed as a teamworking exercise. We've actually managed to undertake similar exercises remotely before, as this was the only workable way of ensuring that all the key global leaders managed to input to the brandscape. But what the remote method gains in individual deep thinking, it loses in spark, energy, and teamwork – pretty important by-products.

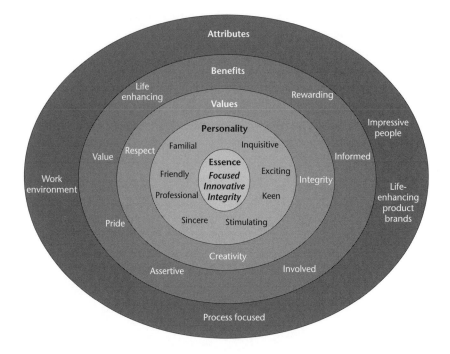

FIGURE 3.14 **Example of a top level brandscape analysis**

The 360 degree research in support of this type of analysis is undertaken with customers, suppliers, and staff alike, who are asked, in a confidential environment, to reflect upon their actual day-to-day experience of the brand. The rigors associated with intensive market research are applied and the research participants constantly updated as to how their input is being used and how the work is progressing (the values of integrity and respect in action were being role modeled in this case).

The last point highlights an important "side effect" of the diagnostic or research phase, namely that the act of asking the questions, the exercise of entering into dialogue sends out important signals, such as:

1. What's important, "what gets measured gets done"
2. The organization values and respects the input of the participants
3. The organization is already role modeling the desired future state (the way we'll be doing things around here in future, the future culture)
4. Open communication is going to be the norm.

With this depth of understanding about the behavioral and values-driven DNA of the organization, we were able to add real "texture" and character to the resultant dialogue about the behavioral components of its five-year strategy. By using this as the centerpiece of a brand strategy development workshop for the top team, we were also able to provide the team with an early opportunity to role model the values themselves, which helped considerably with the ownership and communication of the outcomes. At the fore of these outcomes was a story about the evolution of the business, the foundations of a marketing strategy, and the principles underpinning an employee engagement program, which were all rolled out simultaneously; a first in the organization.

It's no surprise to me that the company concerned has subsequently reported that it has successfully been able to engage with staff, customers, and business partners, to the extent that it has made it into the UK's *Best 100 Companies to Work For* in the 2006 poll. Its mission, brand, and business strategy have been founded on an authentic and clear understanding of its defining brand characteristics, its USP, and, most importantly, improved results have followed.

Brand engagement

Gandhi's famous words "be the change you want to see" (as quoted in Fisher-McGarry, 2006) ring true throughout this process, as there's little point writing a great story about the enterprising brand you aim to be and then pinning your engagement plan to the wall where the only action will be watching the corners slowly curl over.

Even worse, is claiming to be the brand that puts innovation and people first, and is financially astute and yet subsequently blowing the brand engagement budget on away days for the senior execs, and rafts of the marketing budget developing the new livery and mouse mats for the staff, accompanied by a PR campaign demanding suggestions and "creativity." It never ceases to amaze me how much of this nonsense there is about in the market. It smacks of tier two capability and thinking, while facing a tier one challenge. A quick audit of the shelves of the knowledge management function of most organizations reveals the fading slogans of past internal PR campaigns.

But get the approach right and the communication program should really start to gather pace at this point. Following the brand development stage, budget and practicality concerns can mean that the brand awareness phase tends to be dominated by push communication. It doesn't have to be that way. A generous approach to consultation and involvement focused around the brand values can yield energizing and novel engagement suggestions. During the diagnostic, consultation and awareness phases, it is possible and certainly desirable to communicate the sentiments and flavor of the consultation exercise even when time and practicality dictate that mass participation is limited. There is much that the skilled communication team can do to:

- position the context of the story
- formulate a simple but effective creative platform, perhaps road testing the inevitable shortlist of options developed with the creative agencies
- develop an enigmatic teaser campaign to stimulate interest
- liberate the message through innovative and inexpensive use of existing media but focus on role modeling the brand values
- encourage audience participation, stimulating ideas, suggestions, and involvement via less expensive channels like:
  - the existing team briefing process
  - a program of brand development-related corporate street theatre
  - a "diary room" for impromptu feedback and suggestions
  - "open house" discovery and brainstorming sessions
  - anonymous, mediated chat rooms, linked blogs, and so on
  - workshops with a vertical slice of employees from random functions.

These are just a few suggestions and this certainly isn't a definitive list. The additional value of involving a people panel during the strategic phase will be that, if facilitated properly, they will generate their own ideas which will be appropriate for the unique challenge and circumstances of your organization. For guidelines on engagement interventions which are fit for purpose, refer back to Figure 3.9, The engagement staircase.

Contrast the two approaches of organizations A and B. Organization A, a government department, adopted a forward-thinking approach to its brand. Responding to customer and stakeholder feedback, it acknowledged the value of unifying its constituent departments under a single brand identity and associated set of values. Recognizing that it had one last chance to turn the organization around, the board decided to take an active interest and closely manage a thorough process. It undertook a long and deep diagnostic phase to gauge stakeholder perceptions at all levels within the hierarchy; to start the engagement process internally and set realistic stretch goals. It deliberately staggered the communication process to gradually work its way through the engagement continuum. The culmination of the engagement process was a large-scale series of brand awareness and goal-setting presentations and road shows covering all members of staff.

Organization B, an international telecommunications company, needed to undertake a brand refresh following significant changes to the core business in response to market developments. The first step was a brandscape workshop with the top team and three invited employee representatives. This included a raft of customer feedback and employee data, which had been adapted at source to include brand and engagement-related questions. Following the workshop, a picture of the existing brandscape had been shared and a shortlist of brand attributes and values agreed. This was communicated to all staff using the key existing channels but via an attention-grabbing creative platform. Input was requested and volunteers invited for the next stage in the development process. The communication team was overwhelmed with requests to participate.

Organization A represents a rather sad case of control over involvement, thorough process over clear thinking. It attempted to be credible within the existing culture without truly understanding the root cause of the issue and therefore simply reinforced the existing culture. What they said about change didn't matter as their actions were shouting much louder. Despite good intentions, in this case the communication pipeline was a classic representation of Bernoulli's principle, as shown in Figure 3.15.

In organization A, because the communication process was forced through the hierarchical pipeline and most effort was invested in senior communication, the flow of information to the rest of the organization was restricted for quite some time.

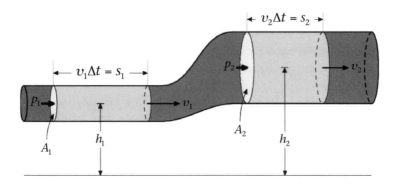

FIGURE 3.15 **Bernoulli's principle and communication flow**

Note: Bernoulli's principle states that for an ideal fluid (low speed air is a good approximation), with no work being performed on the fluid, an increase in velocity occurs simultaneously with a decrease in pressure or a change in the fluid's gravitational potential energy.

Most people weren't actively involved until the workshops, almost a year later, but the communication flow was restricted and instead they started to hear rumors, just a the volume of emotions were rising, about something actively happening to the fundamental identity of their business, began to become concerned about restructures, and were drip-fed by their line managers who were cautious about communicating as they didn't feel they had the answers. Everyone, however, was well aware of the mounting customer criticism of their performance.

By the time most employees were actively involved, the carefully planned progress of the engagement process was overwhelmed by the rush of pent-up emotion emitted by a frustrated workforce; the pressure was palpable, unmanageable, and entirely counterproductive. Subsequent requests to participate in opinion surveys were met with a fair proportion of spoiled questionnaires, and an unsanctioned graffiti board appeared in a communal area, lampooning the process. It frightened the leadership team, who reverted back to push communication and focused most subsequent effort on the senior managers.

Three years later and following a further, expensive wave of culture and brand awareness research, the organization has shown no tangible signs of culture change other than at the very top. It has just been broken up and is being completely rebranded once again at considerable cost.

Organization B, however, had not only involved more people earlier on in the process but had also opened up fresh channels and undertaken an enigmatic teaser campaign called Firestarter. It was channeled through a variety of media from posters and stickers, through to webcasts, impromptu Q&A sessions, competitions and "values theatre" performances by a traveling company of in-house actors. The campaign was informed by a panel of employees made up of a cross-section of staff.

By the time they officially unveiled the new brand at a single event attended by a group of staff elected by their peers, the participants were well past the information-gathering stage and ready to get stuck into full-on experimentation. They suggested a range of pragmatic ways to leverage the brand in the market that are still having an impact on the bottom line. There was little concern about "expected behavior," as they were effectively living the brand by role modeling the values, while employing existing skills and knowledge to work on concepts focused on the bottom line. Quite a difference.

Brand commitment

As mentioned earlier, in this day and age, commitment is a loaded term. It strongly implies some form of obligation, at odds with most employees who expect to shift employers roughly every 2.5 years and who shirk formal commitment in their personal lives. Commitment's close cousins engagement and involvement can be pretty scary too, if pitched clumsily. Certainly, to expect total commitment to a brand predicated solely on a financial contract is pretty unrealistic.

Commitment implies emotional connection and emotional connection is largely driven by a meeting of values, experiences, and reinforced behaviors. The implications for brand managers should be obvious. Be explicit about what your brand stands for in key communication and people processes, target employees and customers who empathize with these values, role model the values at chief engagement officer level, create opportunities for involvement and reinforce this with measurement and you'll be several steps closer to engaging with and hopefully gaining some form of commitment from employees and in turn customers.

WHAT DO COMMITTED EMPLOYEES LOOK LIKE?

Fear not, this isn't the part of the book where we share stories about beaming, beautiful, on-brand people bidding you "have a nice day," nor am I about to lampoon the unsung introverts who quietly get on with the job in hand.

Organizations are made up of individuals as diverse as the wonderful pantheon of human characteristics allows. So how can brand engagement ever be likened to rounding up sheep, getting ducks in rows or herding cattle? Brand engagement is the process of ensuring that the organization and its policies, people, and processes are in harmony with the brand values so that they are geared around meeting customer needs. It's about symbiosis and has nothing to do with alignment.

Brand commitment presents itself very differently in different cultures (a fact that advertisers sometimes forget). As we know, appropriate behavior is determined by the context. It's one of those annoying intangibles: "you'll know it when you see it." But here are a few clues:

- what's your employee feedback data saying about the extent to which employees would recommend you as an employer?
- what would your typical employee say if, in a social context, they were asked who they work for?
- how are your brand values reflected in your people processes, including recruitment, induction, learning and development, performance management, and so on?
- in your immediate team, how many "champions" would you be happy to put in front of a delegation of customers tomorrow?
- how many could name your brand values?
- how often do you celebrate a customer service success?
- how much do you know about your people and do they apply skills they use in their home life in the workplace?

- how many interactive communication forums exist and to what extent are they used?
- are you measuring the "staff as customers" index, that is, if applicable, how many employees are buying your products or services?
- what does your core communication team look and feel like: a buzzing newsroom or a team of credible brand champions?

But remember, employees are responsible for meeting business goals and, to a large degree, this does mean adopting received wisdom, the "way." Being on-brand does not necessarily mean "doing my job, my way" – that's the slow path to creeping brand death. Employees simply have to recognize that their role is to serve, satisfy, and delight customers – and true brand differentiation comes when they do this collectively in a manner that is unique to their organization. An indistinct brand is no brand really. True innovation, however, is more likely to stem from disciplined creativity within the parameters of the brand rather than unbridled chaos. So take care how you position the brand internally, allow people the space to experiment, play, and explore but never loosen your grip on the feedback pulse.

Case Study
ZURICH: INVOLVEMENT-DRIVEN EMPLOYEE ENGAGEMENT

Patrick H. O'Sullivan is currently a member of the group executive committee and chief growth officer of Zurich Financial Services (Zurich) as well as vice-chairman of the group management board. As a consultant, I had the pleasure of working with him after he joined Zurich's UKISA business division, following the merger of the financial services arm of BAT Industries and the Zurich Group in 1998, when he became CEO, general insurance and banking.

Patrick has had a long and distinguished career in financial services. After qualifying as a chartered accountant with Arthur Andersen, he worked for Bank of America in London, Miami, Los Angeles, and Frankfurt; Goldman Sachs where he worked as financial controller for Europe; Financial Guaranty Insurance Company, where he was appointed to the board in 1993; BZW, the former investment banking arm of Barclays Bank plc, where he was head of international banking and structured finance before becoming COO in September 1996; and Eagle Star Insurance Company, which he joined in 1997 as chief executive.

Although he would hate me saying it, Patrick combines the empathic qualities needed to get the best out of people with a well-honed appreciation of the bottom line. He is a firm advocate of teamwork, values-based management, and leadership by example. Like many of the other senior leaders we've discussed, he is proficient in both the technical and behavioral elements of the leadership mix. He's a rare chief engagement officer and CEO package.

He was appointed in the aftermath of a significant merger, which, for a time, left the Zurich brand in factional fragments. The Allied Dunbar brand, for example, was a dominant force in the mix but was characterized in the press by hard-nosed sales techniques, an image that threatened to dominate the merged brand. Patrick's initial goal was to forge a top team based around a common vision, objectives, strategy and set of values and then to unify the business around this core. Unlike many others in his position, he didn't sit in a darkened room drawing up a plan but got "out there" and did a lot of listening, both personally and via his communication network.

Patrick favors gregarious, nonconfrontational communication in his interactions with peers and colleagues and, despite the inevitable territorial issues that characterize merger scenarios, his intention was always to ensure that his top team become the leading brand ambassadors for the new Zurich, the unofficial brand name for his vision. He places great stock in the power of professional internal communication.

Making judicious use of independent external advisers to elicit the improvement feedback of employees, customers, and key stakeholders, he was able to ensure that the information was distilled into an easily digestible format and then used to inform facilitated discussions between the top team. These facilitated sessions were designed to:

- move the group rapidly through the phases of team development, from storming through to norming and on to performing, as effectively as possible
- identify strengths and improvement areas within the group
- engage the group, through personal involvement, in developing a change program that would leverage the benefits of the newly merged entity and outweigh potential "tribal" issues.

This short list was a lot easier to compile than address.

Mergers and acquisitions, especially when accompanied by inevitable new appointments, are fraught with hidden cultural dangers, however compelling the financial and strategic business case. The insurance industry has deep historic roots with proud traditions and in this case, allegiances to the component brands were very strong. Worryingly, these allegiances threatened to slow the required pace of change, as they were manifesting themselves in behaviors that weren't always in the best interests of the wider team.

To help bring about effective top team engagement with the future rather than defense of the past, we developed a business simulation device based on what we call experience engineering principles, and which we termed "Predator." This represented a safe but challenging "third way," a route for facilitating and exploring behavior and a vehicle for facilitating discussions about the existing business but from a simulated neutral territory, while recreating the buzz, energy, and clean sheet of a business start-up. Using Predator, we hoped constructively to reengineer interpersonal relationships and accepted, but not always constructive processes, rituals and norms within the senior team.

The leaders were invited to an unfamiliar, neutral venue for a strategic brainstorming session. This was conducted under the role-playing scenario that they had just left their jobs and had placed their mortgages on the line in order to take up a leading role in the new venture.

This small theatrical conceit, when handled professionally, can be a powerful way of liberating participants from learned conflict and the chattels of tired, reactionary on-brand behavior, when that behavior is out of tune with the times. If only for the briefest of moments in time, it helps the FD, for example, step out of his critical role and connect with his creativity, or the HR director escape the burden of people responsibility and stifling political correctness, just as they probably would if they were running businesses funded by themselves.

As we all know, one of the benefits of a start-up scenario is the chance to throw away the rule book relating to structures, procedures, and roles and create an organization in the image of our "if only" wish list. The Predator exercise takes away the traditional "if only" excuses, replacing them with "what if."

The outcomes from this facilitated process eventually included:

- the core components of a vision for the business
- three key focal points for the business strategy
- three logical key phases in the change program
- an understanding of the role that values, like pioneering, and the new Zurich brand would play

- an appreciation that communication represented the greatest common improvement area and opportunity
- an understanding of and appreciation for the personalities, relative preferences, strengths and weaknesses of the team and individuals
- an appreciation of the role modeling that the respective leaders would have to undertake
- the foundations for an employee engagement program.

The last point included an acceptance that the communication process had already begun. By taking the time to consult key stakeholders professionally, the board was already sending a signal that it valued teamwork and, most importantly, two-way communication, and the questions it was asking signaled what was important in the business. It was off to a rolling start.

The development of the communication strategy evolved over time but was initially based around milestone engagement events, or what I call "totemic communication sessions" to emphasize their "presidential" nature. The prevalent communication culture was sales and celebration focused, based around large-scale, often macho, periodic events of this nature. This had become the accepted way for senior leaders to gather messages and network, but relied on a haphazard cascade, supplemented by reams of centrally generated material created by a central newsroom and distributed through a network of part-time communicators. It was a classic bureaucratic communication model in action.

Rather than cancel the planned cascades, the decision was taken to improve them and to start a multipronged change process and adopt the cascades as change milestones. Responsibility for first phase engagement was shared between the directors and internal communication, while the function received investment to review and refine their operation to become role models for the new Zurich values.

Responsibility for the design of the next three series of major engagement events was brought into the CEO's office and through a collaboration process between the head of organization development and internal communication, the top 250/500 sessions became major staging posts to role model engagement and were focused around the first three phases of the push toward the new Zurich vision and brand. They were to take a values-led approach rather than the usual information push. It was therefore essential that they quickly set an appropriately engaging tone.

THE CATALYST EVENT

Zurich had an indistinct presence in the UK market and the general insurance managers had a relatively low opinion about the ability of their people to think outside the box or the appetite of their peers for brand-based, innovative, funky communication. How wrong they turned out to be. The first event was designed as an exercise in appreciative inquiry, interaction, and positive visualization, and it worked a treat.

In a sea change from past events, where the program was kicked off by the CEO and then rolled out in hierarchical order, this event began as a confidence-building retrospective – the opening act was set in the future and the event was compered by a junior member of staff. Other staff members representing the future employee demographic featured, talking passionately and appreciatively about the origins of the change journey and the conditions that had led to the achievement of new Zurich's goals and brand dominance. It was a simple theatrical visualization device but had an immediate impact. The participants were left in little doubt that the conference signaled a new way of working, demanded risk taking, and a break with the old order. Other acts included:

- Introducing the business case for change (a combination of city analyst data, live customer and staff feedback, competitor analysis, and pan-industry best practice)
- Introducing and obtaining input to the new Zurich vision
- Understanding the three key change milestones and exploring ways in which to address them
- Focusing on the brand values and how the value of pioneering, in particular, holds the potential to drive brand differentiation and competitive advantage.

As the pivotal event for signaling a change in attitude, approach, and style, each of the top team were asked to step out of their comfort zone and play an active role in the process (and not always the role they were comfortable with). The focus was on forward thinking, creativity, and aspiration, and role modeling the previously little explored value of pioneering, the one marked difference between Zurich and the value set of its industry peers.

The whole event was structured to facilitate cross-functional working. Presentation was maintained at an absolute minimum and at the heart of the engagement process was a mass "skunk workshop," where the participants were asked to form a series of mini-Zurichs and, role modeling the pioneering value, teased through a process designed to liberate existing ideas and generate fresh approaches to business. They were facilitated by trained members of their own peer group. Having participated in a similar process relatively recently, the board members mucked in with genuine and infectious enthusiasm.

The energy was phenomenal and the quality of the eventual outputs inspired one of the directors to step forward and adopt the innovation mantle. He gave a personal commitment to take forward the ideas generated as well as to explore ways to create an innovation support process, but, more importantly, to help cultivate a pioneering culture across the business.

Further engagement events

Subsequent totemic events followed and the sequence included focus on:

- *Customer service:* where forum theatre techniques were employed to bring real customer service scenarios to life within a customer arena and collectively reengineer the conclusions in real time with the help of the core values
- *The Zurich live experience:* an appreciative showcase of programs celebrating what the business does well
- *Innovation and pioneering:* the expansion of the business simulation process and the creation of a bespoke series of workshops, designed in conjunction with arts-in-business partners, aimed at liberating creativity and the pioneering spirit. This focused initially on taking the first batch of new Zurich concepts through to implementation, prioritized on the basis of their fit with the most important business goals.

Importantly, the change program was transforming the profile and influence of the internal communications function, which now had consistent presence at the top table. The unit made a gradual move toward a loosely aligned hub and spoke structure, based around a single engagement strategy and standards applicable across the business. Part-time communicators were replaced with full-time professionals with bespoke personal development plans, and a complete revamp of all tactical channels was undertaken and regular stakeholder measurement introduced. A great deal of effort was invested to bring internal communication, HR and OD closer together under the director of operations, allowing Patrick to gradually ease back from a spearhead role as the new brand culture developed around him.

In the four years that followed, the Zurich business in the UK achieved the goals it had ambitiously set for itself and united behind the new Zurich. The brand, with the confidence to take on sponsorship of English rugby union's Premier league, has since become one of the most recognized insurance names worldwide. In December 2002, Patrick O'Sullivan felt able to assume a senior group level role and became a member of the group executive committee, looking to infuse group HQ with his pragmatic engagement philosophy. Interestingly, he took his head of communication with him.

At the same time as Patrick left his UK role, Zurich moved wholeheartedly to a single brand identity and raised customer expectations with a highly public "pigs will fly" advertising campaign.

While this advertising campaign was highly controversial, and much criticized in the press as a classic case of overpromising in an industry notorious for inertia, the internal engagement program was extremely well received by employees, who were still cresting the wave of confident engagement energy and eager to be involved with the brand development process.

An important initial step was a measurement initiative loosely termed "staff as customers," which sought to understand the relationship between Zurich employees and their product. As the employee demographic married with their customer demographic, employee purchasing decisions at Zurich are a valuable benchmark of how they feel about the brand. The initial statistics weren't as encouraging as they needed to be and ambitious goals were set to create a generation of employee-as-consumer brand advocates.

LookOUT road shows

Working with a coalition of people across the business, the time was finally right to break from the pattern of centralized events and we helped the communications team create a more cost-effective and ultimately more inclusive traveling road show. Facilitated by trained, voluntary brand ambassadors, it enabled people to participate in a learning experience based around the notion of individually and collectively delivering a superior customer experience.

Interactive road shows, including one of the first mobile walk-through experiences, reached over 6,500 staff across the UK, involving them in:

- the new strategy (post Patrick) and the Zurich business model
- how the Zurich brand connected all parts of the business in the eyes of its stakeholders
- ways in which they could deliver a superior customer experience, which built loyalty and deepened the relationship with the brand.

The aim of the process was to develop an experiential way of engaging people in:

- the business strategy
- where they fit in
- how the company makes and loses money
- building a "one company culture," where the internal experience of employees creates a great experience for the customer
- defining what a superior customer experience looks like for all the different parts of the business
- how employees will be the leaders of the revolution (a panel of employees co-designed the experience and employees facilitated it)
- providing the real expertise about superior customer experience
- generating pride in the business.

The LookOUT road shows, as they came to be known, did finally culminate in a leadership conference but as a way of responding to and acting on the feedback, suggestions, and ideas (a reversal of traditional notions of cascade). The process deliberately avoided a sheep-dip approach. Attendance was voluntary (although attendance figures were high), but it created opportunities for each employee to explore what the Zurich brand meant to them and how they themselves delivered value to the business.

The LookOUT campaign generated fantastic results:

- internal stakeholder feedback was very positive

- the vast majority of staff responded to an online survey, which contributed valuable ideas for creating the superior customer experience
- significant improvements were seen in staff feedback results, several months later
- employee retention figures were positive, despite structure changes
- major customer satisfaction developments were reported, both as quick wins and gradual improvements
- a number of innovative business solutions were taken from concept stage through to innovation relatively rapidly, employing a mixed team of external facilitators and employees. They have generated significant income to date.

But perhaps the most significant change has been the fact that the Zurich brand has been adopted by the internal and external markets and is now a well-established name. Zurich employees have overcome misconceptions that insurance has to be dull, reactionary, and unglamorous – a necessary evil – but survey results reveal a growing belief that they actually deliver an emergency service when people are at their most vulnerable. More staff now buy their own product. Connecting brand values with personal motivators has liberated this shift in perception and has had significant knock-on effects. It's given Zurich the confidence to raise the profile of its brand and it isn't too much of a cliché to say that it has managed to role model its latest advertising strapline – change happenz.

The Zurich story illustrates the power of brand engagement within the internal market. The challenge now is maintaining the progress and sustaining a change culture in the much criticized financial services industry, notorious for increasingly losing touch with customers and staff.

SUMMARY OF KEY LEARNINGS

The Zurich case study illustrates many of the major learning points of the book thus far:

- the importance of a visionary leader who adopts an appropriate style and simple, clear milestones and goals
- the impact of sharing responsibility for internal communication

- a leader who understands the power of engagement and the business case for employee engagement, focused on the brand
- the power of two-way dialogue
- the power of the story
- the impact that a "follow me" approach by the top team will have
- how a coalition and partnership between the key people disciplines is vital for developing the brand
- the value of an appreciative, respectful approach to managing change
- how values can be a catalyst for culture change
- the need to balance systems thinking, process and behavior change
- how critical the mix between strategic, totemic and tactical communication is for developing a powerful engagement plan
- the role that professional communicators can play
- the energizing effect that involvement-led engagement can have on the business, and the impact it can have on both the brand and the bottom line

5 Things to Try Today

1. Ensure that the internal communication community has a shared strategy and capability across the engagement continuum by linking performance management and development processes to the model.
2. Put in place at least one forum for collaboration across the communication disciplines and focus the forum on a brand engagement goal.
3. Seek out engagement skills development opportunities and start the development process with the top team.
4. Carry out a brandscape analysis with a cross-section of stakeholders and brainstorm opportunities to engage employees more effectively with the brand.
5. Find a way to link brand-related communication activity and budget to ROI.

ACT 4

CULTURE AS A WEAPON OF MASS CONSTRUCTION

DECEMBER 2000

It's halfway through the vision launch for the Top 500. A faceless someone at the podium has just quoted Virgin's Richard Branson saying words to the effect of "a business has to be fun and involving if it's going to bring out your creativity." Pretty ironic given that Everyman's struggling to keep his eyes open. "I guess this means I've made it though," he sighs to himself during one of the many zoning out sessions he lapses into during the day's proceedings. "At least one aspect of today has been particularly useful," he reflects, "I've managed to spend quality time with my team at last, even though most of it's been over breakfast and dinner."

Over another coffee after one of the breakout sessions, he finds himself stuck talking to Jack Hirst (or Mad Jack Hirst as he's more commonly known). It's a real eye-opening conversation. Turns out Mad Jack used to be a drummer for Rod Stewart before he got into this game and has really seen the world from all sides. The reason he gave for putting up such a fight against the restructure was that "I've seen it all before, I could see where it was leading and, for once, I wasn't going to let the machine roll over the right thing." He managed to push through a number of environmental projects as his last act as director. "Saved a load of jobs in his team, but, boy, has he been a pain in the backside in this, his last year. Why go out on such a limb when he could have gone quietly with dignity? Nice of him to offer me his office and personal assistant though, she has a seriously impressive reputation. Not sure what I'm going to do with all those books of his," mused Everyman.

That evening, after the usual speeches and so-called entertainment, he is cornered several times by managers, buoyed by adrenalin, enthusiasm, and bonhomie and looking to boost their personal equity at such a delicate time. Sadly, they included that snake from finance trying to get the jump on this quarter's figures and another entertaining tryst with the flirtatious succubus from PR. "Same rituals, different place each year."

He leaves the bar early to take a last look at the PowerPoint slides for his own trial by podium tomorrow. The lift takes an age to arrive, so while waiting, he calls home and apologizes again for another night away and promises to leave early tomorrow to get a head start on the weekend. He's a bit embarrassed when he realizes that Jack has been sitting quietly, within earshot, sipping a brandy alone in an alcove at the bar. "Nightcap, young man?"

The next morning, Everyman wakes at dawn, refreshed despite the fumes from the cleaning materials, enthusiastic heating system and usual 5 a.m. hotel dawn chorus. He skips breakfast and heads to the plenary room where he's scheduled to speak. He needs to make some fundamental changes to layout and technical spec.

The topic of risk management seems ironically apt, considering his decision to abandon the slides prepared for him by corporate comms just a day earlier. When the CEO emerges with his entourage, Everyman is sitting on the stage in shirt sleeves and jeans and is staring at a sheet containing a diagram showing the organization's values, as if he's only just seen them for the first time. He walks across to the CEO through a scrum of event managers who are frantically rearranging the seating. "Bob, can I have a word with you before the others arrive please?"

WHAT'S CULTURE GOT TO DO WITH IT?

Culture is another loaded word. Marketers refer to power moments in sales situations and in organizational development terms, culture is certainly a power word reflecting a pattern of significant moments and interactions. There's something about culture that remains a mysterious presence lurking somewhere in our business, and managers worry constantly about disturbing it in its lair.

Culture has many complex associations, emotional connections and connotations, and is certainly best approached with respect and care. Reduce the term to its simple descriptor, however, "culture is the way we do things around here" and it's suddenly much more cuddly.

To understand an organization's culture is to begin a process of harnessing and channeling "the way we do things" into incidences and patterns of activity that, ideally, best serve the needs of customers.

After all, that is why the business exists. If the needs of the business are in empathic tune with those of their customers and are delivered by employees who willingly and enthusiastically project a culture in harmony with those needs, chances are the business will be effective, self-fulfilling, and sustainable. That's the power of culture and why it's so important to employee engagement. As we've established that brand management is predominantly a behavioral challenge rather than a process, design and project management technique, culture and brand are inextricably linked.

I've set out to illustrate that effective brand management is the product of an explicit focus on both the physical and behavioral components of a brand. It is dependent on forging authentic partnerships between the internal and external brand stakeholders. It is also reliant upon making connections with the higher order needs of employees and customers alike. Not only is this a formula for authentic brand engagement from a corporate and national perspective but, as we're becoming increasingly aware, brand management is intrinsically tied to issues of global concern.

I've demonstrated that the ongoing professionalization of internal communication and the emergence of employee engagement play a critical part in establishing competitive advantage and that the most important leaders in this process are line managers, not just the totemic figureheads in the business.

To influence culture development can be an elusive and often complex process, but whether you have a blank sheet (as in a start-up scenario), or are working within an organization with a long and deep heritage, the process must commence with the basics:

- an explicit understanding of the business case (why are we doing this?)
- the link to the key goals of the business.

If you aren't clear about these points, don't start out on the journey as you'll never reach the end and will do a lot of collateral damage as you become confused and lost along the way.

A number of years ago I was asked to co-create and run a series of culture and diversity workshops for an international agricultural research company. I was co-delivering at the event, based in Belgium, with the hugely impressive Myrtha Casanova, founder and president of the European Institute for Managing Diversity.

I had been asked to help the international group of senior delegates, mostly male, appreciate why a diversity-led culture development strategy made business sense and wasn't simply a US-led compliance issue. The in-house involvement strategy had struggled to make an impact thus far.

Assisting the HR director, we were eventually able to make a compelling case based on appropriately aggressive logic and case studies from respected organizations. But it wasn't until the groups broke into syndicates and were given free rein to explore diversity from the perspective of their employees and customers that the breakthrough came. One of the delegates, one of the few female managers, made the point that they were focusing too far up the supply chain. They were obsessing about the farmers and corporate customers who bought their products, a mostly male purchasing population. But when Myrtha shared some statistics about the power of women, worldwide, as primary domestic decision makers, the true source of purchasing power became clear. Combine this fact with the additional data about women leading the demand for ethical farming practices and the dark clouds began to lift. The business case for a values and core culture rethink finally began to emerge. They stopped focusing on arm-wrestling with purchasing managers and opened their eyes and ears to the power of the housewife and mother.

If an organization turns its sights on organization culture but hasn't clarified these points about the business case first, and then delegates the process to an internal project manager to begin the analysis (which happens surprisingly often), chances are they're going to get the focus wrong, it's going to be seen as highly intrusive and will be met with discomfort, resistance, and disruption. Think and plan carefully before you grasp culture by the tail.

THE CULTURE DEVELOPMENT PROCESS

To describe the culture of an organization involves collating, tracking, and communicating the flow of energy, patterns, and rhythms of behavior between individuals working within the business, which, through repetition and reinforcement, have become traits, mores, and norms.

The only reason for doing this should be to understand and ultimately reinforce constructive or on-brand behavior to such an extent that it becomes predominant. To elevate the study of culture above the reductive realms of organizational psychologists, or even anthropologists, into a pragmatic and powerful business management discipline, it needs to be considered as an equal partner in the management mix.

A common trait among the organizations I've worked with who have experienced the greatest success in turning around their businesses is a clear understanding of the impact that culture has on their brand and, therefore, the role that culture development must play in transforming their brand. Culture development must become the responsibility of leaders throughout the business, not just the HR function.

I'll shortly be sharing an example of culture development in action, illustrating the fact that culture isn't something you can instruct people to go and do, it has to be co-developed with and experienced by them. But, for the culture revolutionaries out there, first it's worth breaking the culture development process down into its constituent parts (Figure 4.1) and briefly exploring them.

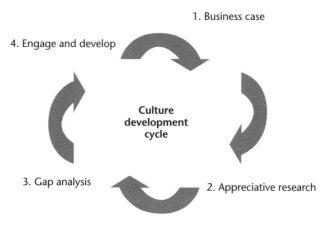

FIGURE 4.1 **The culture development cycle**

Phase 1: Create a business case

Culture change needs to be well thought through. To communicate that you want things to change simply because you have a vague notion that the organization is in some way "unprofessional" is deeply insulting and demotivating. Handle the existing legacy of the organization with great care. Don't contemplate starting the process unless you understand and can clearly articulate why you're doing it and be as specific as possible about objectives.

When the energy company npower stated its intention to focus on culture development, for example, the board was keen to position the process as part of the inclusive program for developing a contemporary vision, which included lofty ambitions for the brand. It was keen to stress existing strengths rather than a gaping performance chasm, an approach that has proven extremely motivating for employees.

Outcomes from this phase include clear objectives signed off by the top team, clear, communicable outcomes, and a simple outline of the forward process.

Phase 2: Appreciative research

This should include work with a representative cross-section of the organization to define and understand the current way things get done as well as to glean clues about the culture required to deliver the business objectives, including appropriate values and behaviors. It's important to do this with the leaders first in order to give them the chance to lead by example, avoid creating an "us and them" situation, and quell any senior-level paranoia and insecurity.

Wherever possible, it is important that an appreciative inquiry approach is taken, with the aim being to explore what's working well, connecting with the core of positive behavior and searching for examples of effective practice rather than simply hunting down problems. The skills associated with appreciative inquiry aren't that dissimilar to the mastery of effective feedback skills; the aim being to convey respect, sustain the energy of the group, and honor the past, as well as understand what isn't working and then moving the organization forward in a balanced but buoyed way.

The key stages in the research phase include:

- *Qualitative interviews* and inclusive focus groups designed with the desired future culture in mind (informed by early contact with the top team)
- *Quantitative research* using a tool like the "organizational culture inventory," or OCI®, which benchmarks culture data using a vast international database, or similar bespoke quantitative research, employing "new media" wherever practical
- *Material culture analysis* in order to understand the impact of the physical environment, symbols and totems as well as nonlinguistic sources including the manifestations of the physical brand.

    This step shouldn't be underestimated. I've seen culture change programs rise and fall on the back of changes to the material culture.

Remember the potency of physical imagery, like the iconic image of the Enron symbol being carted away from its HQ after the scandal broke? The power of physical symbols needs to be acknowledged even if some may perceive them as trivial. Every organization has them and they aren't always obvious. Simple things – like car parking hierarchies, dining arrangements, dress privileges, trophy cabinets, neckties, or furniture signifying rank and even, in one bizarre case, a pond full of goldfish – have all been imbued with a symbolic significance by employees at various organizations, and the way they are treated can impact significantly on the pace of change. So, handle the material culture with care.

- *Desktop research* to collate and analyze the communication assets that are pushed through the mix of normal, day-to-day channels (in-tray exercise, in-box exercise, review of intranet, leaflets, literature including newsletters, briefings and so on) as well as extraordinary items like annual reports, surveys, discussion papers and so on
- *Integrated analysis* to assimilate information and cross-reference data from key sources in order to develop a comprehensive, joined-up picture of the culture and a meaningful story of the culture development journey.

Phase 3: Gap analysis

Gap analysis is understanding the difference between the current and desired culture, allies, threshold guardians, champions, enablers, and potential barriers and working out ways to leverage these characteristics, attributes, and energy centers. In this phase, we commonly use simple tools like the "energy investment indicator," to chart areas of resistance and support brand (Figure 4.2).

Clearly, we all spend a degree of our time in each area but a mark of professionalism is having the self-perception to realize when and to compensate appropriately. The role of an effective leader is to influence the environment and people processes to maximize the time employees spend in the performance zone, to ensure that two-way communication channels are open to constantly understand "where employees are at," and to make continuous improvements to influence the culture. I'm sure we all have our own stories about cynical customer service staff bad-mouthing their own company and can appreciate that if too many employees spend too much time in the bottom half of the four-box matrix in Figure 4.2, the brand will deteriorate rapidly. But is there a more tragic sight than someone who smiles, nods and says the right things yet fails to deliver? How does your current team fare as ambassadors for your brand if you plot their current positions on the matrix? This simple tool has worked wonders in the past as a catalyst for change.

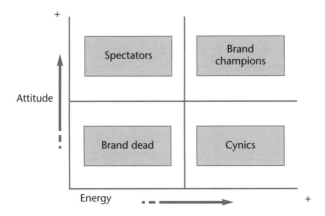

FIGURE 4.2 **Brand energy investment indicator**

Phase 4: Engagement and development

This last phase should incorporate the following elements:

■ *Agreeing a plan of action* for engaging all employees in the change story (why we're doing this, where we've been and where we're going)
■ *Experiential learning opportunities* that demonstrate the desired future culture in a way that charms and attracts employees
■ *Working with leaders* on ways of role modeling the desired way of doing things (this often takes the form of values-based leadership coaching with the leadership team as a whole and one-to-one coaching with individuals)
■ *Hard-wiring key people processes* to support the culture change through explicit reference to the values that constitute the "new way" in recruitment, induction, performance management and communication procedures and measuring the impact
■ *Rolling out a communication program* that exemplifies the new values, works its way up the engagement staircase, and seeks out good news and early wins.

Once again, the communication part of phase 4 arguably commences during the diagnostic or research phase and the importance of the engagement continuum should feature in early discussions. As we know, the very act of undertaking the research is communicating what is valued in the organization.

This process illustrates that the top team must appreciate the impact that the culture development process will have on the organization, commit to lead by example and do all they can to ensure that the process is well positioned, efficiently and expediently run. They must be committed and able to move from analysis of current culture through to developing a picture of the desired future culture as quickly as possible and ensure that the engagement process is informed, as richly as possible, by the desired culture (how can you talk about empowerment as a value and yet only drip-feed information through a rigid, sign-off hierarchy for example?).

Given the importance and impact that culture should have, there is only one true custodian of internal culture and that's the chief executive. The DNA of the desired future culture must be the very structure around which his or her top team is built, which is why a focus on culture development is often one of the first tasks that visionary leaders initiate upon taking office.

Case Study
MOTABILITY: A CULTURE-FIRST APPROACH TO CHANGE

Of the organizations I've had the pleasure to work with in this area, I've made what for some may appear to be an unlikely choice as icon for an engagement-led and people-centered approach to managing change. It's an organization that could well have been hamstrung by its not-for-profit associations and yet can teach most top tier blue-chip companies a lesson or two about managing performance and implementing change. It's a business spanning a number of sectors – including the sales, legal, customer service, not for profit, retail, financial services and motor industry. It's an organization that clearly illustrates the power of culture development as a source of authentic brand management. But most importantly it has achieved a complete performance turnaround in three years.

Motability (Local Employer of the Year and Number 48 in *The Times Best 100 Companies to Work For* in 2007) was conceived in the summer of love, 1977. Motability's founding mission was simply to give freedom of mobility to people with disabilities through providing the use of a motorcar. But before you dismiss its serious business credentials by consigning this case study to the dusty file marked "charity," consider this:

- Around one in 14 of all new cars sold in the UK in the next year will go to a Motability customer
- Motability Operations purchases 167,000 new cars every year (7 percent of all new cars in the UK) and sells 140,000
- Motability Operations has an annual turnover of £997 million and assets worth £2.5 billion.

Motability is actually a close alliance of two organizations, Motability, the charity, and Motability Operations, the not-for-profit organization owned by five major banks (Barclays, HBOS, Lloyds TSB, HSBC and Royal Bank of Scotland) that administers the scheme on behalf of the charity. This is a potentially volatile mix of organizational cultures.

With 600 employees across sites in Bristol and London, this brand manages the largest car fleet in any European country (450,000 plus cars), working with 34 major car manufacturers and with more than 4,000 accredited car dealerships. It has just made the upper half of the UK's 100 Best Companies, in the first year of entry and is in the top five of organizations whose employees believe their organization makes a positive difference. That's quite an achievement, particularly when the competition included some of the most recognizable names in the corporate pantheon (mighty Microsoft made position 35).

I've worked with both arms of Motability since 2001. In that time, I have witnessed a complete turnaround in the attitude and performance of its own people, its suppliers and partners. Having worked with a number of blue-chip, highly capitalized organizations in related sectors, in the same time period, including NSPCC, HSBC, Barclays, Honda, the DTI, BMW, Rover, Ford, and Tata Motors, Motability could teach many of them a great deal about the power of employee brand engagement as a tool for driving innovation and impacting the bottom line.

One of the factors making the Motability story so remarkable is that, throughout its development, it has been true to its founding principles, while competing in a market that is renowned as one of the most cutthroat, macho and margin-sensitive areas in which to do business. Despite inevitable and necessary tensions between the demands of the operations side and the sensibilities of the charity, it has been able to draw on its core values to unite its people through times of change, while developing strategies, a culture, traits, behaviors, and characteristics that have enabled it to become an employer of choice and an extremely commercial force. Never, at any stage, have the greater needs of its customers slipped from the collective mind.

The Motability offering is as complex as the varying demands of its customers (and Motability people are passionate about the term "customer"):

- Customers can choose from over 3,000 makes and models
- 18 different wheelchair-accessible brands are available on the scheme
- Adaptations are fitted to Motability cars by 76 different suppliers in the UK.

Given the problems the average car consumer has in reconciling the various specification options available when making a new car purchase, we can all appreciate that the bespoke Motability offering is complex. The mix of technical expertise and empathetic people skills is a delicate and rare blend.

One of the cornerstones of its success has been to sensitively redefine the perceptions of the users of its scheme, emphasizing that they are customers with distinct needs rather than passive recipients of charity. It's an important distinction, which brings about a particular state of mind and pattern of associated behaviors.

The way the scheme works is that Motability enables disabled people and their families to use, what is termed in the UK, the higher rate component of the disability living allowance (or the war pensioners' mobility supplement) to lease a brand new car. Motability Operations recognizes that not only do its customers have distinct needs, they also have choice, so it works hard to ensure high levels of customer satisfaction. Reinvesting all profits back into the business allows Motability Operations to provide the most desirable and affordable motoring solutions:

- 100 percent of customer applications take place online (with the exception of grant customers and joint agreements)
- There are no waiting lists, credit checks or further assessments required when choosing a car on the Motability scheme

- The most popular adaptations required by Motability car scheme customers, such as push-pull hand controls and left-foot accelerators, are included at no extra cost and over 84 percent of adaptations required by customers are currently available to order from their local car dealer at the same time as choosing a new car.

Despite the complexity of its product, the varying needs of its customers, the power and leverage of its suppliers, and the culturally complex operating environment, 97 percent of Motability car scheme customers would recommend Motability to a friend. What wouldn't most customer service companies give for similar ratings? These statistics are now highly respected by companies in the motor vehicle industry who are clamoring for its business. In fact, two of our existing customers, a major insurance company and an engineering firm, herald the Motability account as an aspirational account target in their change management strategies. That's quite a compliment. But it wasn't always this way.

It's easy to dismiss the 1970s as a decade of heady idealism fuelled by postwar affluence and excess and therefore relatively simple to patronize a business born at this time. It's true to say that, in the past, Motability Operations was viewed with a cynical sneer by some of its suppliers and corporate players within this rather unforgiving, margin-hungry industry. According to one Motability operations line manager:

> We used to be considered a joke by most car dealerships who sometimes took advantage. They thought it was a hassle to serve our customers and certainly believed they didn't have to give us the same service they provided to other customers. They believed that people who worked here did so because they wanted to work for a charity and somehow weren't as professional. We had a reputation in the market as a "soft touch."

If that was an attitude conveyed by some of their suppliers in the past, it's certainly changed now.

What people often forget about the 1970s is that far from being simply a decade of peace, free will and "dropping out," it was also a period of discontentment and rebellion, where seemingly established notions of social order, culture, benevolence, and propriety met a rising tide of antiestablishment energy. It was a time of change. In that sense, Motability is an organization of its time – the product of a charitable heart and soul married with cutting-edge business nous. Foremost among a group of forward-thinking leaders, Mike Betts, CEO of the operations arm, has been both visionary bridge builder and rebel in chief. Stretching the 1970's analogy a little further, he's a little more Hendrix than David Cassidy at heart.

Mike, whose earlier career included over 10 years' experience in the car leasing industry and several years at Thorn EMI (latterly as operations director for Thorn EMI Business Communications), was appointed CEO of Motability Operations in 2003. Before this, as Motability Operations' chief operating officer, he was responsible for developing and implementing a substantial change program aptly called Together.

During Mike's tenure, he has overseen a series of achievements that have helped Motability Operations become a leading player in the car market. Pointedly rejecting overly complex accounting matrices, Mike has trenchantly persisted with a simple but balanced portfolio of measures (Table 4.1).

TABLE 4.1 **Balanced portfolio of measures**

Finance	Customer
Cost reduction	Customer satisfaction/referrals
Underlying profitability	Customer renewals
	New customers/growth
Internal quality/process management	**Organization development/people**
Core process management	Culture development
Process efficiency	Employee engagement

The Together program was engineered to ensure that the organization centered first and foremost around customer needs. One of the initial steps in the process was to commission an internal culture audit process to understand the preferred style of operating, traits, norms, and relationships between the respective employee groups and management teams. By adopting an approach and range of tools that provided pan-industry benchmarks, Mike Betts was able to draw clear and objective observations about the strengths and shortcomings of the internal culture. Needless to say, in the process, the line management community emerged as a pivotal community, where the existing culture mix was at its most intense concentration.

The next step was to work with his leadership team to understand the business priorities, the part that culture, values, and behaviors could play in addressing those priorities and then articulating the desired future culture needed to best serve the needs of customers.

Following an extensive process of sharing the outcomes with key colleagues and stakeholders, internal values (the three Fs), and behaviors were developed in consultation with customers and colleagues. The objective was that these values would then encourage behaviors in line with the desired future culture and bring to life the Motability Operations brand internally and externally. By focusing the leaders on a simple series of performance metrics and this powerful set of core values, Mike has been able to ensure that, in turn, employees are effectively engaged with the core goal as they are rewarded for behavior that is on-brand.

These measures and values provide the focus for a series of integrated work streams around customers, people, technology, and efficiency.

Motability Operations: Our Values
Friendly
Flexible
Facilitating

As part of the process, Mike and his team also focused on and then transformed the external brand identity to ensure that the physical manifestations of the brand – including imagery, color palette, livery, logo, and strap line, and their delivery via key channels – echoed the core mission, values, and ideals. Importantly, the process of addressing the physical aspects of the brand was explicitly led by the change program and informed by the core values and culture – never the other way round.

The name changed to Motability to reflect the evolving nature of the business and to help coordinate and harmonize activities between Operations and the charity and to reflect a more holistic and customer-centric offering. All customer-facing materials came to share a single creative platform and approach.

The company also undertook a substantial overhaul of the physical premises, following feedback from the material culture analysis part of the consultation process. It updated and professionalized the communal spaces in order to reflect a belief that treating staff with respect will have a rapid knock-on effect for customers. This was a difficult task to undertake at a time when the organization was being resized. Clumsy positioning of the exercise would clearly attract a great deal of criticism and impact morale but customer and employee feedback suggests that it clearly worked.

From this

Motability Finance Limited

to this

Despite having to make significant adjustments to staffing to reflect the refocusing of priorities and improved processes, the company counterbalanced the inevitable negative impact on morale with a complete overhaul of vital people processes like performance management, competency sets, training and development opportunities, and pay and benefits. The key was to ensure total transparency in support of the customer-centric goals and performance culture and to send out a strong message about the new performance culture as it generously rewards customer-centric achievements.

A comprehensive reengineering of internal and customer communication was also undertaken, with the redesign of all essential channels in light of the brand values, ensuring greater access to the top team and insistence on a more professional approach to running the team, with the greatest emphasis placed on line manager-driven communication.

Recognizing the importance of leaders role modeling the change they want to see, Mike's early steps of consultation and listening, conducting scores of reviews with customers and suppliers, and undertaking several inclusive culture audits set a precedent for continuous assessment and improvement.

Just as Motability Operations wasn't always taken seriously by the motor industry, it's fair to say that the organization hasn't always been an employer of choice. But it has worked hard to overturn these impressions of its employment brand. It now offers an extremely competitive package and a great deal of credible internal development opportunities. The company has made a series of high-profile appointments at senior levels and in key positions, many headhunted from respected, related industries. In addition, it has recently been active in the graduate recruitment market, giving talks at Oxford and Cambridge recruitment events, for example. In this respect, it is well ahead of most of the recruitment industry, recognizing and catering for a growing demand among potential employees who want to make a difference and are seeking more from their employers than just a great financial package.

Most importantly, the Motability Operations employment brand caters to this growing demand for what may be termed "ethical employment," while competing at the commercial cutting edge. As one employee puts it:

> You used to join Motability Operations when you were nearing retirement age or were tired of competing; now it's seen as a place for high performers to get great experience and to build a career.

Having worked closely with its leadership team, it is clear that the people factor has been central to the company's success. As leadership is probably the critical success factor in any change program, one of the most important actions Motability took was to develop a set of culture-related leadership behavioral indicators, based on the outcomes of the independently administered culture work. In the first instance, all leaders incorporated these into their performance assessments, followed (once they had become accustomed to the process and inspired by role modeling) by all employees. As ever, the truism that "what gets measured gets done" applies.

But what about chief engagement officers? Very early on, Motability recognized the pivotal role of line managers as cultural "lightning rods" and deliberately focused a great deal of early engagement effort on this core community. The resizing process inevitably started here to signal the changing shape and nature of the business.

Leaders are now selected largely for their people skills rather than technical ability, which called for some difficult personnel changes early on in the process. As well as company-wide people surveys, there is now a 360 degree feedback process to ensure that values-based management is alive and well, and the process includes input from colleagues, line reports, customers, employees, and business partners.

Recruiting, equipping, and engaging with people at Motability are all clearly critical. In the past, it focused on compliance-led administrative and technical skills and sometimes promoted people based on how long they had been doing a job and because of their experience gained in affiliated industries (many recruits were taken from professional services). Of course, these qualities are still important but a big change is that the Motability Operations employment brand now prioritizes customer-focused core values and attitudes.

A people strategy based around leadership, reward, recruitment, on-brand working practices, and authentic communications has greatly helped the Motability brand get to where it is now. According to the survey undertaken as part of the Best 100 Companies process, 82 percent of employees at Motability Operations believe that the organization is run on strong principles and 81 percent of people working for the company are proud to do so. Despite the market in which they operate and the commercial pressures of asset management, it ranked 11th out of 100 for profit not being the only factor driving the business and yet its performance metrics are heading steadily north.

The other side of the looking glass

As well as insisting on extremely high standards of service from colleagues to ensure that employees deliver on the brand promise, Motability Operations has invested significantly in the training of the dealers who deliver its car schemes. It trained over 12,000 delegates in 2006 and, just as it believes in engaging internal stakeholders, it now runs key communication events and forums for suppliers throughout the UK. In March 2006, it decided to acknowledge superior performance among its suppliers and partners by establishing an annual supplier awards ceremony, handing out accolades to the likes of Perrys Motor Group, Vauxhall Motors Group, Ford Retail UK, and the RAC for sales, growth, support, and innovation. This is another fine example of a joined-up approach to brand management, this time through understanding and collaborating with the industry culture in which it operates. It also sends out some very confident signals.

In some respects, the Motability brand engagement story is fairly unique. Motability was, first and foremost, founded as a charity and despite the fact that Motability Operations was created separately and is owned by a number of banks, the more passive/defensive characteristics associated with traditional notions of charity used to dominate the culture. But the indicator on the culture barometer is now firmly stuck on constructive behaviors. Yes, it's possible to affect change at the top by dramatically changing the team but, remarkably, the most significant culture shift at Motability happened, not just at the top, but right across the business within the first two years of the program.

All activities at Motability Operations are still carried out in line with the UK government's objectives to improve the lifestyles of disabled people and yet it now operates successfully in a notoriously competitive commercial environment. It explicitly puts customers and staff first but has a rapidly growing reputation for assertive supplier management and for negotiating extremely commercial deals.

The cynics could point to the government grant aspect of its balance sheet and the fact that the nature of the business should make it easier to engage employees compared to the average profiteering corporate. But the Motability heritage has certainly been a double-edged sword. I would argue that, in light of this not-for-profit heritage, it has been a tougher task for the Motability team to make difficult people decisions and reengineer its internal culture to ensure the optimum balance between emotion and logic, hearts and minds.

Motability Operations has worked hard to ensure that it replicates the hard-nosed commercialism of its market, particularly in terms of the expectations it sets for its partners. Testimony to its success has been the fact that it now attracts key staff from its main suppliers in the car and leasing industries.

Motability is arguably the most successful organization I've worked with in terms of the culture-led performance turnaround it has achieved in a relatively short timescale. Far from allowing benevolent cultural complacency to set in, it has recognized its uniquely dichotomous position, embraced it, and developed it into a USP.

Compare this story to the amorphous offerings of many major automobile organizations, leasing and financial services companies and even charities, which look to differentiate themselves first and foremost through marketing and advertising. What wouldn't they give to ensure that their people, processes, and even products are consistently able to deliver on the promises made by the brand?

We could all learn something about brand management from Motability, but let's hear from a customer:

> I am on my fourth Motability vehicle and things have really improved over the years. Combined with my wonderful Motability

dealer, the whole process has been so effortless. Motability is the best thing since sliced bread. (quoted in *Radar*, the magazine of the Disability Network, 2006)

THE USE OF TOOLS

We all love a gimmick, a gadget, a liberating device. Clients clamor for something they can package up and use at their discretion. When dealing with slippery issues like culture development, tools, whether bespoke or market standard, sometimes help to provide rational islands on an angry sea of change. Our communication professionals talked earlier about the obsession with technological solutions and new media, but we also explored how media is really no substitute for sound methodology. Earlier, we also talked about Kubrick's iconic movie *2001* when making the link between brand, behaviors, and a good story. Just as HAL, the supreme tool, was ultimately outmaneuvered by mankind's resourcefulness, survival instinct, and ability to improvise, culture development isn't something that tools and gimmicks alone can facilitate. But their objectivity certainly helps to drive clarity and insight in what is an emotive field.

Culture analysis calls for a blend of sound, insightful and involving qualitative analysis and thorough, inclusive and credible quantitative analysis. This should include the use of employee surveys (incorporating existing tools and data wherever possible), but true benchmarking data is invaluable when looking to understand and address culture. By far the most established and credible tool in the market at present is the "Organizational Culture Inventory"® (OCI) tool, which I have used as part of my work with a host of clients over a number of years, including Motability. There are many other tools that I personally use regularly, some of which I shall also refer to in this section.

About the Organizational Culture Inventory®

The Organizational Culture Inventory® (Figure 4.3) is the most widely used, thoroughly researched tool for measuring organizational culture. Twenty years of research into organizational culture, its causes, and its outcomes allow the owners and comprehensive database administrators, Human Synergistics®, in conjunction with accredited consultancy partners, to identify current culture outcomes at the individual, group, and organizational levels. It also identifies the specific levers for change that must be addressed to change culture.

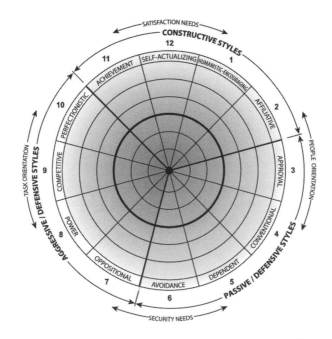

FIGURE 4.3 **The Organizational Culture Inventory**®

Source: Research and development by Robert A. Cooke, Ph.D.
and J. Clayton Lafferty, Ph.D.

The OCI® contains 120 statements that organizational members use to describe the behaviors, activities, and customary mode of operation that characterize their work environment and relationships with others. The OCI® measures "what is expected" of members of an organization, or the behavioral norms and expectations associated with a given organization. This analysis helps to define the current culture.

The OCI® can also be used to measure the "ideal" behaviors in an organization; the behaviors and expectations "that should be expected" from members of an organization, to create the best possible (that is, most effective) organization. This is known as the "aspirational" or desired future culture. Ideally, both current and desired future culture analysis should be undertaken by the leadership team as early on in the culture development process as possible.

When completing the OCI® about the current culture, organization members are asked to describe the behavioral "styles" they are expected to adopt in carrying out their work and when interacting with others:

- The *constructive* cluster (11–2) measures the extent to which members are encouraged to interact with people and approach tasks in ways that help them to meet their higher order satisfaction needs
- The *passive/defensive* cluster (3–6) measures the extent to which members believe they must interact with people in ways that will not threaten their own security and do things "by the rules"
- The a*ggressive/defensive* cluster (7–10) measures the extent to which members are expected to approach tasks in forceful ways and to protect their status and security (Figure 4.3).

The analysis is presented in a circumplex (Figure 4.4), which provides a snapshot of perceived behavioral norms for the organization as a whole, subsections and departments, offices, and by key constituents of the organization's demographic.

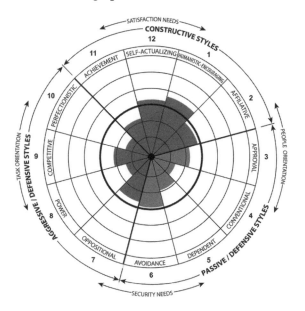

FIGURE 4.4 **The OCI® circumplex**

Source: Research and development by Robert A. Cooke, Ph.D. and J. Clayton Lafferty, Ph.D.

A host of illustrative data comparisons are available, showing the profiles for high-performing cultures across different industries or to compare culture profiles within and across industries (Figure 4.5). There is a strong emphasis on fitness for purpose in the analysis,

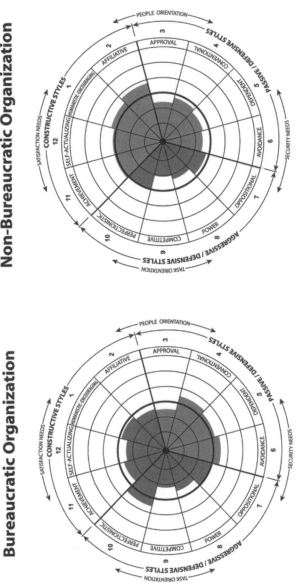

FIGURE 4.5 **Culture profile for a public sector and a private sector company compared**

Source: Culture profiles from *Organizational Culture Inventory Interpretation & Development Guide*, Human Synergistics International (2003)

however, as, while constructive styles are clearly seen as aspirational, leaders need to make decisions about the appropriate culture needed to achieve their future business goals. In Motability Operations' case, "Into the blue" (the colour of the constructive cluster), became a popular and powerful rallying cry and after two years, it transformed its internal culture. For more details about the OCI® and Human Synergistics'® associated suite of tools, refer to www.human-synergistics.com.

A selection of other bespoke culture and engagement tools

The folk at Infinite Resources, one of the boutique organization development consultancy firms within the BY2W Fellowship, have developed a tool called Impact (Figure 4.6) to help line managers engage more effectively with employees as part of the performance management and development process. The Impact tool can be adapted to fit the competency and behavior framework of individual organizations but the core purpose remains the same. It provides a snapshot of the participant's leadership style by gathering 360 degree data, working through this in an interactive but automated process and representing this graphically to benchmark and chart preferences, strengths, and improvement areas. Simple but effective, it has proven extremely successful in helping sensitive healthcare Trust employees make the link between their own competencies, values, and behaviors and the goals of the business.

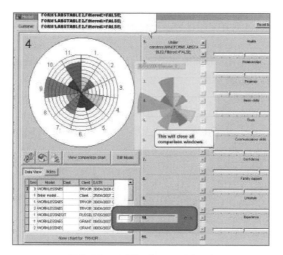

FIGURE 4.6 **The Impact tool**

Accompanied by interactive workshops to explore individual and group contribution contrasted with organization need (whether focused on organization or brand development), this type of tool can have a significant influence by providing a consistent, seemingly objective process, common terminology and point of reference, and a visual representation of complex behavioral traits.

On the tactical communication side, we've developed something akin to an air traffic control tool called the Radar, which is aimed at identifying and managing the volume of tactical message generation and helps communicators to spend a greater proportion of their time focused on strategic value added and behavior change.

FIGURE 4.7 **The Radar tool**

Again, if placed within the context of a wider engagement strategy and plan, the tool can be extremely useful in helping communicators to develop team and individual capability across the engagement continuum. The tool isn't an end in itself and certainly can't replace core skills development, but it does remove one of the barriers to effective engagement.

As an extension of the visualization techniques employed in workshops and other face-to-face, information-gathering sessions, our colleagues at visual communication and design agency blue goose have developed "Cue Cardz" (Figure 4.8). They've proven to be a powerful and versatile associative thinking, learning, and development tool, which can be used as a five minute icebreaker, an interactive and stimulating one-off exercise, or the central focus of a bite-sized workshop when combined with appropriate facilitation techniques. Small but perfectly formed, they're entertaining engagement in action.

Darumas (Figure 4.8) are spherical dolls with a red painted body and a white face, but without pupils. They represent Bodhidharma, the founder of Zen Buddhism. It is Japanese custom to paint one of the doll's pupils at the beginning of a new year, make a wish and paint in the second pupil, if the wish comes true. In a technique taken from Japanese kaizen or continuous improvement philosophy, darumas are given as gifts to accompany skills development or goal-setting initiatives and play on our natural inclination toward synergy and closure (we ache to paint in the second pupil); quirky and slightly bizarre they are nevertheless gentle, provocative reminders to focus on an objective we've set ourselves or deliver on a promise made.

FIGURE 4.8 **Cue Cardz and daruma**

There are plenty of creative tools out there in the marketplace which can help in the brand engagement journey as culture development catalysts and we've developed a number of bespoke tools for clients ranging from board games based on the hero's journey through to process-reengineering role plays to develop critical thinking capability. The important element is to encourage stimulation of the range of senses and encourage engagement by making the culture development process energizing, entertaining and involving. These are just a few of our favorites. In the final act, we explore some of the most effective ways of role modeling the principles discussed in this act by examining the part that storytelling, mythology, and the arts can play in stimulating involvement in the interests of lasting brand engagement.

SUMMARY OF KEY LEARNINGS

- Culture development is an essential part of the employee brand engagement process. I would suggest that so-called intangibles, like culture and behaviors, constitute as much as 80 percent of the makeup of a brand. They need to be handled with care but to avoid them is to bury the head (and the heart) of the brand in the sand

- Culture development inevitably requires behavior change. The change management process has to be centered on people, rather than focused on the process as a means in itself

- There are a variety of approaches that can be taken to culture development but two principles should take precedence: leaders have to spearhead the process and the process itself must role model the change you want to see

- Judicious use of models and tools can certainly help to stimulate engagement but they can never substitute for a comprehensive values and behavior-led engagement program

5 Things to Try Today

1. Map the key stakeholders in the brand engagement process and chart them on the energy investment model, reflecting how they embody your brand values.

2. Develop a bullet point strategy for creating a business case for culture development and start the process by selling it to the top team.

3. Draw up a shortlist of key people throughout the business to involve and engage in the process, who will co-facilitate.

4. Enlist the help of an independent, trusted adviser to co-create the culture development process.

5. Involve the communication coalition in drawing up a comprehensive employee engagement plan that role models the values.

ACT 5

BRING YOURSELF TO WORK

If the work you're doing is what you chose to do because you love it then it may well be your bliss. If not, then it's your dragon.

(Campbell, 2001)

Tim Bulmer (2007) *Lowry retrospective or just another day in paradise?*

APRIL 2006

Everyman has finally married. It's a lot later than his parents did (and the decision had nothing to do with their constant reminders), but he likes to think it's all the better for the wait, and will hopefully last a lot longer. "Who was it who said that men shouldn't even consider tying the knot until at least 32?" They have a young family (scandalously started out of wedlock) and, as they have both battled to maintain a footing on their respective career ladders, are helped out by a full-time nanny and a punishing schedule of structured activities for the kids. It seems there just hasn't been enough time to kick a ball around in the park anymore, so something has had to give.

Grateful for the loyalty the corporation has shown him, but finding the living patterns and needs of family life increasingly incompatible with corporate life, Everyman has, after a long discussion with the family, recently taken the decision to start his own business venture, working from an office at home. He'll miss the bonhomie but won't miss the rituals of travel, meet and travel. They come to collect the company SUV tomorrow.

A City solicitor has bought the place next door and turned it into one-bedroom flats. "Shame the builders plowed up the front garden to make parking spaces." The local area doesn't have much real community feeling now and, tired of worries about schooling, car parking, crime, and congestion taxation, they have decided to sell up, follow a dream – one that appears to their friends to have come from nowhere – and move to the country. "They all think we're mad moving to a village that doesn't even have any shops," he muses quietly to himself, as he tucks in his baby son's blankets and turns up the Mozart adagios on the iPod. "But how much stuff do we really need?"

"Entertainment technology, where would we be without it?" he whispers, looking into the digital baby monitor. Admittedly, gadgets have made it a lot easier to connect with colleagues when they can't be in the same place, and it's easy to keep up to date with new developments when your nephew keeps you on your technology toes, but he also remembers how long his father resisted the first in-car phone, "the only time I get any head space," he used to mutter.

Recently, a late-night conversation led them to track down long-lost friends through an online social network. Turns out that one couple, who they haven't seen since a friend's wedding in the late 1990s, live quite close to the village they're moving to. They've all grown older but still sound the same and he's looking forward to exchanging war stories over a fine bottle or two.

Everyman started a correspondence course some time ago, and, buoyed by the encouragement, has taken up writing again. He has just bought a new bike with the proceeds from a golf article. An early triumph. The knock-on effect of this new hobby has been to dust down those old novels filed away in the garage. He's just finished rereading George Orwell's *Keep the Aspidistra Flying* for some reason, "Strange writer, Orwell. Visionary in many ways but lapses into caricature in many others. I never understood why Gordon Comstock threw away his life's work, at the end? Moody sort of a bloke."

Just then, his Blackberry buzzes. Only the news headlines, usual stuff about housing prices, war on terror, and "fat cat" personal equity scandals. "Make a good fairytale one day," he laughs quietly to himself and then, on his way out, turns off the bleeping machine: "someone else has booked a story this evening."

EVERYTHING BEGINS WITH A STORY

The heading is actually a partial quote taken from an interview with storyteller, mythologist, and maverick professor Joseph Campbell (1904–87). The study of literature, drama, and epic narrative teaches us that there is an innate rhythm and structure to great stories, the recipe for engaging communication. We're all familiar with the rules. It's inherited wisdom, social consciousness gleaned at bedtime while battling heavy eyelids. We're gently nurtured to love stories and it's easy to forget that, long before we invented the means of capturing stories mechanically, the important and symbolic tales were passed down orally through the generations. It's a skill as old as the ebb and flow of nature. So why isn't great, engaging, face-to-face, involving communication the norm in even the stuffiest of organizations?

In the eternal pantheon of stories, there's a core conceit epitomized by the central character, the hero, the figure who represents all of us. The hero embarks upon a journey in response to a catalyst, a significant event that summons him to adventure. The hero's subsequent journey concerns the search for an antidote to a dilemma that his community, his society, is facing. This search becomes the quest to fulfil a compelling want, it draws the hero away from the community and, reluctantly but inevitably, he embarks on a voyage of discovery, transformation, change. During the journey, he has to face a series of trials and archetypal characters that test and transform his ways of doing things; they explore and exploit his values, his morals, and his integrity. The journey opens his eyes to the wisdom of new ways and alternative perspectives, until finally he returns, a transformed person, and proceeds to introduce change to his community. I'm sure this resonates with stories from your social reference points but does any of this sound familiar when you consider your experiences at work?

Think hard enough and you'll recall the structure of the story. On reflection, you will also recall that the fate of the hero is played out in the context of three outcomes or endings: the tragic, the comic, or the heroic. Just as the hero has to decide to embrace the call to adventure and respond with courage, a combination of his own actions, the choices he makes and the gradual unveiling of providence will ultimately determine which ending will be his fate.

Where there is a tragic ending, it's a reflection of the fact that the hero does learn during the trials of the journey but ultimate wisdom arrives too late (think *Othello, Brazil, The English Patient, Spartacus*). Where there is a comedic ending, the hero changes somewhat but never really learns and is fated to repeat his mistakes (think the core conceit in *Groundhog Day*, Bottom in *Midsummer Night's Dream*, Inspector Clouseau in the *Pink Panther* movies). But a heroic ending arises when the hero journeys, endures his trials, learns, changes, and returns to his community with an answer to the compelling want, something which he is part of and which has, in turn, changed him irrevocably.

The trial represents a process of surrendering something of himself (often a type of death), in the service of others. The hero becomes self-dependent in the process, exercises free will and chooses to return to serve his community rather than simply drawing from the community as he did before.

On reflection, we can doubtless recognize the patterns, themes, and outcomes. Hero archetypes are represented everywhere in our culture, most obviously in the output of the arts and entertainment industries. The story structure is central to all the major religions, it informs our games, our teaching, and, more recently it is used to encourage us to buy things.

But what is a corporate change process if it isn't a hero's journey or epic change saga in its own right? What's a brand or a vision launch for that matter or even the process of starting out on a new job? The motifs in the story, the hero's journey, are as relevant to us now as they have always been, regardless of our sophisticated communication tools. In fact, facing up to the global challenges we're now confronted with is going to require a return to heroic references.

But as Campbell (2001) puts it: "We're not entering the journey alone, the heroes of all time have gone before us."

Joseph Campbell refers to "the hero with a thousand faces" to reflect the cross-cultural proliferation of a similar story. In turn, he refers to mythology as "stories people tell to make sense of the universe and their place in it," and the brain as "a secondary organ," a rational system which must eventually submit to "an inner humanity, a spirituality." I would assert that mythology and storytelling hold the keys to helping chief engagement officers navigate the maze of organizational change. This may be a little too rich for the blood of certain "dyed in the wool" corporate consciousnesses, who have to believe that corporate methodology is somehow divorced from culture and that rational self-determinism is the only clear path. But even the most ardent separatist can relate to the fact that people are fascinated by a good story; that they're motivated by more than cold logic; and perhaps they can also appreciate that they could learn something about engagement if they suspended their disbelief for a moment.

MYTHOLOGY, THE ANCIENT ARTS AND EMPLOYEE ENGAGEMENT

Decades of business literature have brought an enlightenment of their own but have also contributed to an obfuscation of certain essential truths. Conversely, we may be entertained and attracted by story-tellers, welcome arts in business companies into conferences as a cathartic distraction but, let's face it, a large percentage of the working population still feel uncomfortable letting the artistes through the revolving doors. "It's too intimidating" or "just isn't serious enough," the critics cry. But they're doing a great injustice to what we've come to call the arts, which collectively represent a lore far deeper rooted in what makes us all "tick" than the comparatively recent phenomenon of corporate "business think."

I'll readily admit to being pretty uncomfortable myself when, suited and booted, I've had to endure a poorly contextualized Native American Indian "talking stick" brainstorm or a random free expression, drumming and musical teamworking event, when, quite frankly, I had more pressing issues on my mind. On reflection, however, a lot of my reaction had to do with the positioning of the exercise or reluctance, on my part, to commit myself fully to that community. Two very different but associated issues.

But let your own mind wander back through a few historical references and you'll recall that the worlds of commerce, politics, faith, and the arts have been entwined for as long as we can recall. Long before most people could write, 11th-century troubadours entertained and educated with tales of chivalry and gallantry; court jesters provided satirical catharsis and critique literally at the seat of power; and in ancient Greece and Rome, plays and dances were carefully constructed to flatter, criticize, soothe, or deceive. The famous play within the play in *Hamlet* is a perfect example. What was Hamlet's answer to the taboo of regicide?

the play's the thing wherein I'll catch the conscience of the King.
(*Hamlet, Prince of Denmark*, 2, 2, 633)

Of course, Shakespeare, at a very dangerous time for artists, was holding up a mirror to his contemporary society, the play within the play within the play. He himself was once again using art to an end that surpassed the superficial. Art is and can be used in the same way within corporate kingdoms today as a constructive way of enhancing communication, involvement, and, ultimately, engagement. But someone has to grant access to the kingdom first.

I would go so far as to assert that the kings and queens of industry have had a longstanding love/hate relationship with the maverick power of the arts, often typified by resentment and distrust. It's hard to reconcile this seemingly anarchic medium with the discipline needed to control a business, a change program or a major improvement drive. Or, as one senior manager put it at a recent conference, confident that he was speaking for a fair proportion of his peers: "I didn't go to business school to have a bunch of unaccountable creative types tell me how to run my company."

While they do make excellent agents provocateurs, it's also fair to say that many representatives of what we can loosely term "the arts" struggle with notions of commerciality and the arts in business industry doesn't have the finest reputation for developing lasting, pragmatic solutions that impact the bottom line. In fact, unless there is a true partnership based upon clear terms of reference, they can sometimes make a bad situation worse. But it's up to the client to ensure that engagement solutions proffered are centered around skills development and skills transfer rather than seemingly stroking the ego of the artistic mentor (personal applause, after all, is why many people enter the profession in the first place). The answer lies in introducing the excitement, involvement, and creativity of the drama but without extended overreliance on the expensive external catalyst – a "third way" somewhere between all or nothing, where personal appearances can then be focused on judicious bursts of catalyzing creativity, the preferred and most effective use of expertise.

For this "third way" to work, it does call for subtle bridge building between the creative arts and "business think." It also calls for a blurring of the stark distinctions we've been encouraged to make between the work and home persona.

The fact is that no matter how sophisticated or sanitized the business, no matter how complex the challenge, the stories, the lore, whether we call it corporate or not, essentially remain the same even though the context and content differs. No matter how intelligent and learned we may consider the audience to be, we can never reinvent the core mythologies, the source material that has actually helped to define the very business cultures and ultimately the societies we're looking to influence and then improve. But we can certainly add to the pantheon of stories, even heroic ones.

It's my view that the wisdom of people like Campbell is extremely relevant to the business arts of engagement, culture development, skills development, leadership and change management, because it stems from a life's work dedicated to uncovering the mysteries of storytelling, spirituality, and mythology across cultures. Campbell is compelling because he understands the lore.

There are a number of reasons why employee engagement can benefit greatly from understanding and applying mythology:

1. The structure and rhythms are essentially the same
2. The rules of engagement are the same
3. The journey maps to the leadership process of self-discovery and sacrifice
4. The characters and motifs are very similar (emotional and political intelligence, archetypes, threshold guardians supporting or challenging and so on)
5. The audience is instinctively attuned to the structure, rhythm and beat, and, with the hero, readily draws lessons from the journey and expects one of three familiar outcomes
6. People crave communication that relates to higher order needs, particularly when their baser needs are largely addressed
7. We are all, at some point or other, interested in the notion of legacy
8. It's a way of uniting the largely rational "outer" corporate change journey with the often emotional "inner" change journey we all take.

How else can you explain the success of the Brazilian spiritual writer Paul Coelho? Despite the fact that English isn't his native language, the author, most famous for his 1988 book *The Alchemist*, has inadvertently become a business guru with a passionate following, despite writing what literary purists may well call naive art. Coelho's colourful use of metaphor and explicit handling of the storytelling genre evoke strong emotions in his readers, who've made him a phenomenon and one of the most influential living writers. *The Alchemist* is a classic hero's journey.

Another book that has taken this particular path, but this time for more explicit corporate use, is *ZAPP! The Lightning of Empowerment*, which fuses the business book and storytelling genres. Written for line managers by Bill Byham with Jeff Cox, interestingly in the gluttonous late 1980s, it unexpectedly became a bestseller and was heralded by *The Wall Street Journal* as the book that "redefined the genre of business books." The legend runs that the book's success came when employees clamored for their own copies after managers started to share its "back to basics" methodologies with them and the messages clearly struck a chord. Initially a self-publishing success, 275,000 copies were sold before commercial publication. This independent stance combined with a simplistic, storytelling style has given the book an iconoclastic brand all of its own. It has now sold several million copies worldwide, paving the way for books like the incredibly successful and equally enigmatic *Who Moved My Cheese?* by Dr Spencer Johnson (co-author of all-time bestseller *The One Minute Manager*). Highly reactionary employees at the Royal Mail, for example, took the core messages to their hearts when asked by their leaders to explore the emotive subject of change. Johnson's book, accompanied by empathic facilitation, was a simple, non-threatening but effective way of moving them through the emotional change curve, helping to explain and contextualize the emotions they were feeling in a way that no genre business book could have. Given the increasingly militant tendencies of their workforce currently and the rising tide of industrial action, their business leaders would be well advised to re-read their copies.

Compare these quotes about Johnson's work:

I'd just learned our board had unexpectedly decided to sell the company. With no assurance of continued employment, I was depressed and playing a serious game of self-pity. Then I read *Who Moved My Cheese?* The book's message hit me like a lightning bolt! I quickly went from being angry at the unfairness of my situation to being full of confidence and keen to find my new cheese. (Michael Carlson, president, Edison Plastics)

I can picture myself reading this wonderful story to my children and grandchildren in our family room with a warm fire glowing, and their understanding the lessons in these important pages. (Lt. Col. Wayne Washer, Aeronautical Systems Center, Wright-Patterson AFB)

By comparison, what would your own grandchildren make of David Maister's latest offering at bedtime? It's no criticism of David, one of the world's leading authorities on the management of professional service firms, to say that you'll certainly learn a lot about your personal engagement skills if you try.

Clearly, I'm exaggerating to make my point but there's more than a grain of truth hidden in the jest. Through the use of classic storytelling techniques, parable, and the judicious application of metaphor, these books don't take themselves too seriously and teach profound truths in bite-size chunks. They appear unthreatening, unintimidating, engage with the readers by reconnecting with the art of play and are, frankly, entertaining. It's an approach that clearly works for millions of people. Among those millions are probably your most important ceos.

Consider the storytelling structure running through this BY2W version of Joseph Campbell's hero's journey, depicted in Figure 5.1, for example.

Now consider this outline for an actual CEO's presentation to his leaders.

1. The business context (our heritage, our current performance, our strengths, our culture)
2. Stakeholder analysis (shareholder, customer and employee feedback)
3. The change imperative (the competition, the industry, the opportunity, our weaknesses and blind spots)
4. The vision and change goals
5. The change journey (time frame, milestones, next steps)
6. Critical success factors
7. Syndicate SWOT exercise
8. Plenary presentations (who's with me and how will we engage our people?)
9. Measurement

The latter is a perfectly logical and thorough structure, which most senior leaders would be proud of. It is focused, well sequenced and has flow. Every point inadvertently relates to Campbell's simple story-telling structure but has been translated into "professional" parlance, corporate speak. Unfortunately, it somehow resulted in a dry, 60-page PowerPoint presentation (I imagine you're picturing the scene as we speak, and I'll wager you're pretty close to the reality). So which approach are you most familiar with? Which has the most immediate appeal? Be honest, which would be the most engaging?

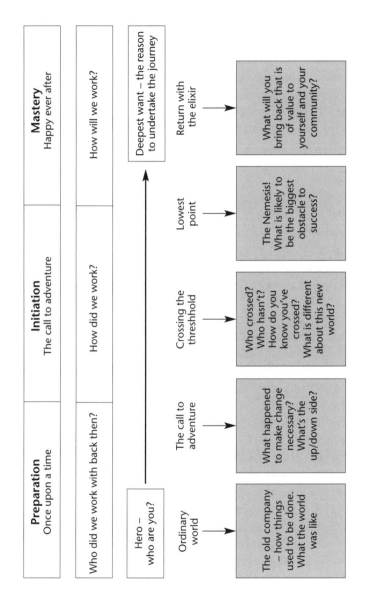

FIGURE 5.1 **The hero's change journey**

Of course, we would all listen to the CEO with interest. He's supposed to say important things and he's probably the alpha status figure and therefore commands our attention, but even though he has tried hard, the CEO's speech is less about involvement and more an exercise in awareness building and confidence development. The thought process is: "I know you're all looking to me for answers, I've spent a long time working on them, and here they are. You're expecting a lot of content. Now what do you think, because I want to make sure no one dissents and I need to understand who can really hack it here?" It's the wolf of push communication in the sheep's clothing of involvement.

It's not easy being at the spearhead of an organization and yet still have the confidence, competence and, most important, patience to open the floodgates to involvement. But in our modern society where people expect empowerment and need to understand the rational, corporate journey but demand to know how this fits with their personal development drive and crave opportunities to express themselves, involvement is the blueprint for engagement. Isn't it somehow heartening to know that, as chief engagement officers, regardless of level, whatever the complexity of the situation, the story has been a constant throughout our social history and whatever the enormity of the change challenge, "the heroes of all time have gone before us"? Isn't it also about time we invested a little less effort reinventing and a little more time listening for the natural rhythms we're all so instinctively in tune with? Surely the modern leader has to be a great conductor, orchestra member, as well as a courageous solo artist in his or her own right?

That certainly seems to be the message coming from the brand guardians, employees, judging by the way they respond to well-facilitated, face-to-face involving engagement activity in particular. Gone are the days when information cascades culminated in conferences at the end of the process as a necessary evil. Reinvest the money you would have spent, on creating a culture of continuous two-way dialogue by developing skills and dynamic procedures that facilitate dialogue. The possibilities are endless but, in recent times, we have co-developed a host of highly involving, innovative engagement forums in partnership with clients. Here are just a few examples:

- *Customer arenas* employing live forum theatre as a way of enacting and reengineering customer service and employee–employee scenarios rather than wading through critical reports

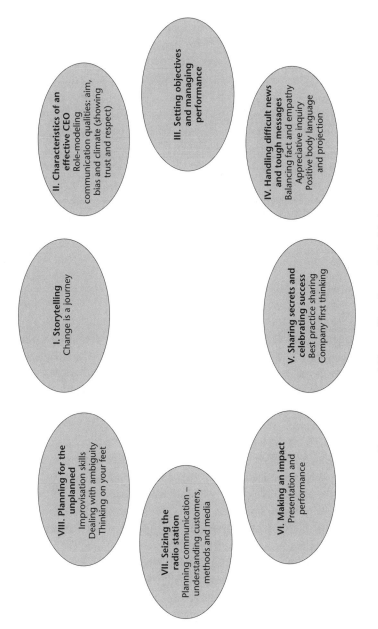

FIGURE 5.2 **Engagement skills profile of a typical chief engagement officer**

- *Involvement-dominated workshops* geared to bringing brand values to life using experience engineering techniques, the exact opposite of publishing papers, giving presentations, and developing models
- *Skills development programs* geared toward the full range of competencies associated with the communication/engagement continuum
- *Storytelling forums* and sensitive, bespoke personal impact coaching rather than power presentation skills training run by walking egos with attached mouths
- *An innovation hothouse* providing a permanent, evolving creative workshop in which new business concepts incubate, supported by a blend of sound process and a culture of inspiring behaviors all facilitated by in-house brand champions.

Many of these concepts have been developed on the back of ideas volunteered by employees rather than so-called creatives. If they're co-created, they're co-owned.

THE STORY OF GOOD COMPANY

The origins of Good Company, a highly successful engagement forum, predate the concept by at least two years when we were asked to assist in the culture-led turnaround program of a well-known financial services brand. Its chief executive was an advocate of communication as a driver of employee engagement and after we had helped to develop a simple but inspirational vision and brand engagement plan with the top team, the next phase in the process was to increase the pace and depth of employee involvement in the transformation process.

Good Company owes its conception to the enlightened engagement approach by the board who had experienced the potential of dynamic engagement activity themselves and wanted to open the eyes of their people to the potential; explicit feedback from customers and the perceptions of employees and brand stakeholders. Using a variety of communication media, we collected a colourful spectrum of perspectives about the corporate brand and used these voices to bring the business case for a more comprehensive and substantial engagement strategy to life.

The Good Company concept was born out of the interplay between a coalition of partners (a foretaste of what has since become the Bring Yourself 2 Work Fellowship), spanning the change consultancy, arts in business and venture capital worlds and blended with process management and technical specialist expertise from within the client business. It became a brand within a brand, a company within a company, for an exciting 18-month period.

Fuelled by a pipeline of focused ideas and innovations that had been generated as a result of a high-profile culture change process and associated communication drive, the objective was to establish "proof of concept," namely that innovation is the sum of good process, relevant culture, values, motivators, and behaviors. Bottom line benefit was the ultimate arbiter.

With the full backing of the board, a sequence of experiences was devised to:

- create and roll out a business simulation and creativity process involving all key leaders
- develop the idea-to-market process
- unleash the creative potential of the participants
- create an ideas bank
- identify and entice talent and champions
- bring the voice of the customer into the room
- develop an experience or ideas pitching approach
- explore the values and behaviors associated with an innovation culture and role model them during the process.

Freed from the daily conventions and rituals of financial services sector behavior, the effect of implementing the phases in the Good Company process was liberating, inspiring, and, ultimately, extremely commercial, earning rapturous reviews from the senior leaders and delivering a number of significant customer-focused innovations. It made a substantial contribution to the business turnaround process and, despite rocky patches along the way, remains a fine example of true collaboration between the creative communication partners and the business stakeholders themselves.

To illustrate the unnecessary conventional dichotomy between work and fun, I'll call upon another famous scene from Terry Gilliam's film *Brazil* where the sinister manager Mr Kurtzman is disturbed in his grey factory of an office by the sounds of cinematic gunfire? When he throws open his office door to investigate, shouting for his deputy Sam Lowry, contrary to his suspicions, the general office of clerks is a hub of normal industrious activity. Meanwhile, behind his back, his personal monitor switches from the figures he's been working on to a classic Western movie.

Returning to his office, the moment he closes his door the movie resumes on the monitors in the general office and the clerks once again grind to a leisurely halt, totally engaged in the movie now on their monitors. The scene repeats itself several times over, the manager, Kurtzman growing increasingly paranoid and agitated with every iteration. As the viewer we're complicit in the subterfuge which is revealed to us whenever Kurtzman opens and closes his office door. It's a memorable parody of the "us" and "them" mentality and the way we've been conditioned to view work and leisure activity as polar extremes. It also illustrates how, despite even the most draconian of regimes, the human spirit of rebelliousness and mischief in pursuit of some form of involving interaction will out. The concept of Good Company is a way of bridging both worlds, leaving the monitors on yet enhancing the productivity the Kurtzmans of the world crave.

But if you really can't relate to the Kurtzman dilemma, if a Good Company process as a way of creating, generating, and sustaining an innovation culture is simply a step too far for your company just now; if the Predator business simulation program is too great a risk for the top team; if the hero's journey concept is more likely to be consigned to the *Star Wars* appreciation society and you can't spare the resources to develop the engagement skills of your leaders, what exactly are your chief engagement officers in residence going to do to connect your corporate vision, culture development dreams and brand values with the key motivators of your employees? They better be very good slides because that video explaining the latest advertisements has probably been in the customer domain for several weeks already and really isn't going to go down very well when it's finally shown at the team briefing meetings.

AUTHENTICITY AND ENGAGEMENT

A core hypothesis throughout this book is that people are more effective when they are undertaking activities that fulfil their higher order needs and work with or for organizations or cultures that exhibit and pursue the same or similar value sets to themselves. At BY2W it's what we refer to as the personal performance zone. Some may say this is a romantic pipe dream. Having spent many years working in the people-centered consultancy field, across a range of industries, I know for a fact that it makes sound business sense.

The implication is that individuals, in the main, have more integrity, sincerity and are generally more authentic when in the home environment. This in turn leads to greater fulfillment and satisfaction, provided they are able to nurture their higher order needs at home. If, however, we have to work for someone else, as most people do, the worst-case scenario is that this relationship between needs, drivers and fulfilment is subsequently undermined at work during the process of trying to earn a living. Some people call this compromise. I call it lazy, short-sighted leadership, which is having a profound impact on the way brands are represented in the market.

People are more effective in the workplace
where the *work* me and the *home* me meet.

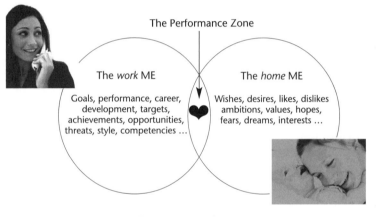

FIGURE 5.3 **The BY2W perfomance zone**

It is a fact that disillusioned, disenchanted employees deliver poor service. Whether you're in a restaurant chain and the waiter bemoans the fact that head office are useless, so your poor quality meal wasn't his fault; whether you're in an interview and the interviewer has no idea about the organization's values, but can quote the expenses policy chapter and verse; or you're flying in a plane and the baggage handlers haven't bothered to carry out the security checks properly, or the cabin crew are on strike because they have been forced to work shifts that don't suit their families, employee engagement and brands are inextricably linked – which means the organization simply has to connect with employee needs and values.

Employees don't always rebel openly, though. It's dangerous to show aggression and speak up and most have to protect their lower order needs, do they not? But this perceived disconnection between value sets is one of the reasons why employees protect themselves by adopting an on-brand mask. For as long as they're able, they present the prevailing culture with what they believe that culture finds useful. If the culture doesn't resonate with their core values, they exhibit behaviors that they feel protect them, a passive/defensive disguise. This clearly isn't maximizing the potential in the relationship and will ultimately undermine the brand, as the mask will slip from time to time (or when Kurtzman turns his back). If there's genuine and sincere culture fit, however, it's far more likely that authentic engagement will be possible and that the brand will be the stronger for the support and the fit. The shift from passive/defensive to constructive behaviors was the biggest single factor in the Motability success story.

For example, some time ago we were asked to run a series of workshops with senior employees from a government department. The aim was to understand how to improve employee engagement within the department. On the face of it, according to the manuals, performance management literature, and so on, its people processes were sound. But, owing to a series of very public incidents revealing a breakdown in the relationship between senior and middle managers, our objective expertise was sought to try and understand the discrepancy between their processes and recent behaviour and get to the root cause. We were happy to help yet the client insisted on stringently controlling the design process, engagement process, and information-gathering methodology.

Needless to say, although no one dissented openly, the first diagnostic workshop was like "pulling teeth." We had to work extremely hard to break down barriers, largely by focusing on the seemingly neutral territory of impromptu exercises designed to understand the employees as rounded individuals, reflecting on their personal values, home lives, interests, and achievements. We also had to go to extraordinary lengths to contract with attendees that all input would remain confidential and had to reinforce this by refusing the client access to raw feedback material, despite persistent demands. This was only the initial fact-finding workshop and we were already at the very heart of the engagement problem.

The ultimate performance zone is undoubtedly in the region where the "work me" and the "home me" meet, provided the organization and the individual can connect with and complement each other. This is why brand values and people processes like recruitment, induction, communication, development, and performance management are so vital. Much of the work of the effective chief engagement officer should be spent uncovering and exploiting this common ground, certainly if he or she is to engage with internal stakeholders in an authentic and lasting way rather than measure success by completing tasks, bums on seats, and pushing output.

But isn't it rather ludicrous that terms like "work–life balance" even exist or that we ask ourselves questions like "do I work to live or live to work?" It wasn't that long ago that junior executives were thought to be "on brand" if they reinforced the first part of that sentence. Where did the notion originate that, to exhibit our natural characteristics, to show emotion, was somehow the same as "acting unprofessionally"? Surely this is a serious hangover from the bureaucratic command and control model of organization design and is tragically "out of time." Shouldn't we have evolved a more compatible and empathic model of working by now?

THE JOHN LEWIS GROUP: AN AUTHENTIC BRAND

When the much respected retail brand John Lewis, which also owns premium supermarket chain Waitrose, announced handsome profits in 2007, the public reaction was hugely enlightening. One well known commentator, an otherwise cynical satirist and comedian, was quoted as saying with all sincerity: "I'm very pleased. Whenever I'm feeling down and disillusioned with life, I pay them a visit and somehow find my faith restored." But it isn't just John Lewis's customers who were pleased. On the same day, it announced that it would be reinvesting its profits by paying its partners (their term for employees) an 18 percent pay rise across the board. Little surprise that John Lewis employees are consistently mentioned as exemplary brand ambassadors. Now contrast that with the bank staff who read recently that just one of their directors had allegedly been paid an all-time record, eight-figure bonus while many support divisions received virtually nothing. What impact will this have on general customer service, I wonder?

John Lewis is applauded for its core philosophy of "labour employing capital, not capital employing labour." The "partner" tag isn't a platitude as it has a longstanding and well-known key principle of "sharing of knowledge, sharing of power and then sharing profit with staff." Sir Stuart Hampson, its former CEO and chairman, states with confidence that "staff feel motivated, valued, they understand their relationship with customers" and this translates, quite explicitly, into a superior customer experience. It is not a brand of Wal-Mart proportions (who is?), but how many employees would trade places?

It helps the brand that John Lewis has a written constitution first drawn up in 1929 and can trace its operating platform back to its original values. More important, however, is the fact that it has maintained this bond through regular improvements like an internal culture "refresh," a communication and consultation process involving all its 55,000 plus employees.

The lesson here is, if you have a legacy, treasure and use it. But it doesn't take almost a hundred years of history to get there. Cut to the core of star brands like Virgin, Pret A Manger, Starbucks, First Direct and The Body Shop and there's a clear sense of core values and a passion for both employee and customer feedback.

So what makes an authentic brand and why should it matter?

It's important to mention here that an authentic brand won't necessarily be a universally popular brand, even if it's extremely successful in its field. The point is that the brand identity is so clearly defined that we're under no illusions as to what the brand stands for. As long as the brand delivers against that identity in a consistent manner for both employees and customers, it can be considered to be authentic, whatever we think of the nature of its business.

Authentic businesses understand themselves, they are explicit about what they believe, and strive to develop relationships with staff, suppliers, and customers in a manner that is consistent with these beliefs. This kind of branding liberates customers, employees, and stakeholders to make choices about the brand based upon genuine understanding:

- Authentic brands are clear about what they stand for – their core values
- They are clear about what they will stand for, what they will tolerate – the behaviors expected of their people
- They are explicit about the types of customers and employees they want to attract.

If you visit IKEA, there really is little point bemoaning the self-assembly part of the deal, when the goods cost half the price of what they are available for elsewhere. This was a problem for IKEA when it first expanded into the international market but its success has been based upon developing rapid brand awareness and educating stakeholders about what the brand stands for and what it doesn't.

The consumer is liberated to make a choice between price, quality, contemporary design, fashion, and, ultimately, how they choose to invest their time. Potential IKEA recruits can expect similar clear choices. The contrasts between the John Lewis and IKEA brands are vast but they are united in the clear way they position their respective brands, both internally and externally, and in the clarity of the relationship they enjoy with internal and external stakeholders – and so it's no surprise they're both phenomenally successful businesses.

Internal communication, and latterly employee engagement, have arguably become core managerial competency areas in the last decade or so and are major drivers of authenticity. In 2005, Bring Yourself 2 Work conducted a cross-sector survey involving around 1,500 "chief engagement officers" (people in line management roles, regardless of seniority, who are responsible for engaging staff in the core goals of the business). When we asked the question, "what characteristics define an 'authentic' business?," the following unprompted adjectives topped the feedback poll:

- trustworthiness
- genuineness
- reliability
- explicit values.

Importantly, however, when we probed the link between characteristics and reality, the survey showed that:

- 89 percent believe people are more effective when they can be themselves at work
- 91 percent believe that they would be happier if they could be themselves at work.

But only 60 percent believe that being themselves at work would help rather than hinder their career prospects.

What does this say about the communicator's perceptions about the people they work with (their internal customers)? Indeed, what does this say about the culture of the respective organizations? Even within this senior and highly informed population, it's clear that, in at least 40 percent of cases, the culture of the organization is at odds with the true identity of its people, at least to some extent. This, they tell us, impacts career development and as career enhancement is the third biggest determiner of employee engagement (according to Melcrum), this insecurity must ultimately affect sustainable business performance. The difference between the espoused values of the organization, the culture in practice, and the values of employees represents an authenticity gap that many customers will ultimately fall through.

How can employers bridge the authenticity gap?

Absence of clarity relating to individual and corporate values contributes to a growing schizophrenia in the workplace. Lack of authentic internal communication makes it difficult to buy into an ideology when the story unfolding differs from the story told. Uncertainty makes it tricky for employees to trust the organization enough to be themselves and thereby inhibits their performance and ultimately that of the business.

I firmly believe that organizations that communicate in an authentic and engaging fashion are more likely to encourage their employees to volunteer the motivation and innovation that result from them being themselves in the workplace. We've seen this hypothesis reenacted many times. Engaging communication is not cascaded information, it is generated through interaction and happens at all levels.

As with many things in life and business, back to basics is often best. We've found, in coaching scenarios, that this simple authenticity test helps to focus the mind when corporate life becomes complicated.

---

1. **Why are we in business?**
   On the back of an envelope, describe your organization's vision/mission/statement of purpose, what the brand stands for and four of the organization's key goals.

2. **What type of company are we?**
   In five bullet points, list the organization's core values and any associated behaviors.

---

3. What type of colleagues do we have?
Off the top of your head, name 10 senior individuals who are true role models for those values.

4. What's it like to work here?
Imagine you're interviewing a new customer or staff member and explain how those values really relate to:

- day-to-day work
- your brand
- your current advertising
- your internal communication (including face to face, written and electronic)
- your induction and performance management process.

5. What's our story?
Describe the story of the brand, where the organization has been, where it is, where it's going, the part it plays in society, and how you fit in.

6. How are we doing?
List four ways in which staff, customers, and suppliers are involved in shaping key decisions and are consulted about how things are done around here.

How did you get on?

AUTHENTICITY IN ACTION

When working with the senior population of a leading petrochemical company, we were aware of the high degree of cynicism about the command and control language associated with the brand alignment and conformity movement, which had been driven from the corporate HQ, right from the top. Change management and skills development initiatives run by program offices and modeled on "one size fits all," compliance-led interventions were, at best, generating international competitiveness born out of fear. Fragmented local initiatives were taking the place of improvements across the organization as a whole and while some involved minor incidents of brand creep relating to the brand livery, others were potentially placing employees and customers in compromising, even life-threatening situations.

A mismatch of values, poor culture fit, and breakdown in internal communication were compromising the brand, regardless of an expensive advertising campaign, again driven by the center. It was leading to a lose–lose scenario for employees and employer alike, largely attributable to a gaping authenticity chasm. Employees had frankly lost faith in the custodians of the brand, they switched off when faced with internal communication and, to a significant extent, were just focused on trying to get through a day at the refinery without incident.

As trust between the leaders at the center and line managers had been undermined, the last approach the group would have tolerated would have been a clinical, rational, didactic process. They needed to be consulted, listened to and given an opportunity to address the credibility leaks in a brand they essentially had a lot of passion for. They also needed an independent sounding board, as distrust for HR, who were seen as the agents of the establishment, was rife.

By adopting the concept of the hero's journey as a common tool for explaining and exploring the organization's heritage, as well as its potential legacy, with mixed groups of line managers, we were able to penetrate beneath the sterile layer of rational, stock answers and tap into the emotions of the hardened leaders and supervisors, create a common ground in development workshops and overlay the personal experience of senior leaders. Change was gradually perceived as part of the evolution of the organization, a "call to adventure", a personal responsibility as well as a corporate goal that applied to them all rather than something imposed from the center. And because the process allowed us to explore the organization's and individuals' core values from a different perspective and ensure that the participants felt valued and in control, it was easier to gain contributions and shared buy-in to a road map for the future.

Although this involving, gentler approach to engagement was a calculated risk, the engagement process was highly effective because it provided a neutral but involving territory to explore the issues and answered the key questions about legacy, values, culture, goals, and engagement from both a personal and a corporate perspective. The local leaders felt listened to, respected, and found the interaction an uplifting experience. Most importantly, the method role modeled the strategy. It has since become a successful template for wider employee engagement.

Time and again, in what Pine and Gilmour have called the "experience economy," this type of link between performance and culture has been proven. There's little doubt that, particularly in an age when social consciousness is growing, authenticity can drive competitive advantage. So why not try a different way? In our experience, those companies that have truly made their very human values live within their organizations are ultimately the employers of choice, with nothing but positive impacts on the bottom line.

The joint architect of this successful story is an important player in the employee engagement field, my colleague Paul Miller. I've worked with Paul for some time now, but he's enjoyed a distinctly more colourful past than most. In his time, Paul has been an England gymnast, acrobat and circus performer, actor, writer, trainer, philosopher, husband and dad (not necessarily in that order). He is also a much loved facilitator and respected coach and is, himself, on a perpetual journey for balance. He's therefore rather uniquely positioned to comment on the notion of authenticity and being yourself in the workplace and says:

> I've had the rare experience of having been both an international sportsman and a businessman, and, perhaps not surprisingly, the question I'm most commonly asked is: "why are sportspeople so motivated compared to their corporate counterparts?" My answer is simply that sportspeople generally love what they are doing. Sportspeople are always chasing a dream, in a world where their dream makes sense, because their peers share the same dream.

> Jumping over a bar might seem a pointless activity to some people, likewise trying to get a white ball into a small hole situated 400 yards away, but to the person engaged in the activity, it is a passion with endless subtleties. But don't confuse this love with enjoying every minute of the journey. Athletes will endure grueling training schedules and huge sacrifices because they are drawn by a compelling future, the idea of mastering something beyond the reach of the vast majority – something that is beyond the reach of themselves in the present moment, but which they yearn to accomplish.

> This "love/passion" covers a lot of the bases that make for a satisfactory life/experience. As mentioned, sportspeople belong to a group of like-minded peers, they gather self-esteem along the road, they are challenged, they get fit, they get to travel, they are tested and measured (they know where they stand in the world), they can even gain fame and fortune, and may even get to pass on their passion and skills. Of course, there are some sportspeople who thrive on the desire to grind their foe into the dust, but that's not all there is to it – notice how boxers hug their opponents at the end of a fight.

Even sportspeople who don't make the world stage – sportspeople who hold down full-time jobs – share this passion, and this passion is tantamount to a relationship. The relationship is sometimes love/ hate, sometimes sunny and sometimes rocky, but in the end they stick with it because it's a relationship that gives them a clear sense of purpose – something to believe in – and more than that it gives them the excitement of being alive. The leaders in the story were like that, they just needed to remind themselves why they were doing the job and how they could address the challenges both they and the organization faced.

I believe that all people can feel this way if they are engaged in an enterprise that truly turns them on, be it serving in a baker's shop (I've met such a person), running a training department (I've met a number of them), providing a service during a time of dire need, or being CEO of a charity (I've met him as well). Everyone seems to accept that this passion, this tenacious thirst to achieve something or express one's self is prevalent in the arts, sports and even science, but to most the idea of loving your job to such a degree is ludicrous … well, is it? I beg to differ.

The love and passion that Paul talks about is certainly something which can infuse both the work and home worlds. But if this is to be the case, employers will need to encourage it. Employees, in turn, will have to get in touch with their personal values and focus on development beyond the realm of lower order needs, if they're to achieve a vocation that will resonate with loftier aspirations that they currently may not fully understand. The separation of the social context from business is a relatively modern obsession. Where we've erected divisions between the two worlds, we've created buffers between our rational thought, our values, our emotions, and our conscience, and this impacts significantly on the performance of the brands we represent.

BECOMING COMFORTABLE WITH THE EMOTIONAL DIMENSION

We're all fairly familiar with corporate clichés like "winning hearts and minds" or "having the right spirit." There are places within every business where, in fact, we expect emotional hyperbole – it has become the internal brand. Sad, really, as this has meant that emotions are largely compartmentalized and have succumbed to bathos and caricature.

The men are from Mars, women are from Venus gender lobby will suggest that this is a by-product of male-dominated hierarchies. As a product of post-feminism, I find this an irritating oversimplification, because I've had the pleasure of working with many men in touch with their feelings, as the clichéd phrase goes, as well as many stoic or highly competitive women. Emotions have, however, undoubtedly been emasculated, but by bureaucracy and the tyranny of logic and process more than anything else. It isn't just a "man" thing or a hang-over from militaristic bureaucracy models of management. Emotions are unpredictable, can be difficult to control and therefore are poten-tially threatening to a leadership trying to maximize performance. But they're also the route to true engagement. It's a tricky conundrum.

Interestingly, if you extend the comparisons with the world of sport, if someone is said to possess heart, or spirit, they are seen as a true warrior, someone with character, art and bravery, a captain among sportspeople. So why doesn't this always translate to the corporate world?

As we've heard, performance in sport is the result of a development journey that takes commitment, emotional investment, and time. I believe that the pressures placed on senior corporate leaders, however, encourage a short story mentality. There isn't enough focus on the journey of the organization because successive leaders insist on a rational focus on their own hard deliverables, their vision and mile-stones, and "the here and now." If you remove the context from the story, it ceases to be a journey and simply becomes a tableau represent-ing the rational and contractual needs of the leader. A sense of short-termism encourages focus on time-based deliverables at the expense of long-term commitment. There just isn't the space for emotional connection at a level other than at the base of the needs pyramid, the realm of subsistence and conspicuous but basic needs, where mass consumerism lurks.

The arts, on the other hand, represent ancient structures, rhythms and patterns, which resonate with higher order emotions, spirituality, if you will. This is one of the reasons why arts in business initiatives are so well received in the emotion-starved corporate arena. The balance needs to be addressed in the business world, for the following reasons:

- the hunt for spirituality is a natural human impulse, it is in our DNA, in all mythology, and we feel lost without it

- it's a higher order need, a mark of our evolution; if we condition employees to be achievement-focused, employees will demand progression in the development opportunities they have access to and the way they're engaged with the business
- spirituality can be a genuine USP (as in the brand India debate). By unleashing the emotions that feed it, we're servicing something competitors will find hard to emulate.

I'm acutely conscious that these words are being written by a pragmatic, rugby-loving former banker. But there's no embarrassment in an argument in favor of balance when it makes very good business sense. A representative at The Royal Bank of Scotland, with whom I've had a long-standing relationship, estimates that UK firms alone are poised to waste around £365 million on hiring graduates who plan to move on to another company within two years. Those are just the tangible costs. This statement is a mark of fatalism, they don't believe in the ability of employers to connect with, engage, and empower the new generation of graduates. It's not a bad start to the business case for more engaging communication based on stimulating a core passion for addressing higher order needs.

In order to develop that communication, employers must:

- represent the organization's development as a continuum, a journey
- be explicit about values and behaviors, and connect with emotions
- recruit employees with core values in tune with their own, and who genuinely bring themselves to work.

If you need further assurances have another look at the Motability and ARM Holdings stories.

This search for a core passion is what Joseph Campbell calls the search for "bliss" and perhaps it's about time that the cliché-riddled, macho terminology and overt rational dominance of the corporate world was toned down in favor of a return to a more emotional form of expression. Unless we start to understand the power of emotions, be they hidden within corporate values or in the secret passion of totemic leaders, how can any employment brand, let alone corporate brand, have sustainable authentic appeal?

As I've highlighted throughout this book, engaged employees can have a powerful impact on brand performance, but there's a growing body of evidence that, if faced with less than effective communication, employees are starting to take action, even though it's not always explicit and the short-term impact on the brand is sometimes hard to pinpoint immediately. Consider these reflections by David Broome, the associate director of VMA Group and a senior recruitment consultant, commenting on one of the key sectors, the internal communication recruitment market.

WHAT'S BEEN HAPPENING IN THE RECRUITMENT MARKET?

In conversation with an industry expert

IB: How would you describe the development of internal communication as a profession over the last decade or so?

DB: As an executive search and selection consultancy specializing in the communications industry for almost thirty years, we have closely monitored the development of the internal communications profession. Having grown its own internal communications practice, VMA Group itself has reflected the phenomenal growth of the profession in terms of the number of practitioners and internal communications opportunities we represent.

The profession is still a young one in comparison with its PR or marketing cousins. Many organizations are coming new to internal communication as a professional resource in their organizations, with senior internal communicators increasingly seen as vital in engaging and mobilizing employees. HR, which was one of the more traditional repositories for employee engagement, is increasingly seeking out professional support as internal communication has increased in sophistication from simply pushing messages in pursuit of compliance.

As organizations start to understand the strategic value of internal communication, so the internal communication job market has grown and developed to reflect this. The demands of the job have changed but so too have the demands of the internal communication jobseeker.

IB: What impact does physical location have?

DB: The job market in the UK is still dominated by and centered around the capital city, London. There are similar patterns abroad. VMA Group conducted a survey of the internal communications industry in autumn 2006. Of the total of 639 professional internal communication specialists who responded, over 56 percent were based in London or the southeast, with the northwest and Scotland the next most represented regions, at 8 percent and 7 percent respectively. That's a significant bias.

Of course, this reflects the fact that the City still dominates as a site for the corporate HQ (where the internal communication hub is most likely to reside). For many corporate candidates, however, London does still provide a major draw.

The public sector tends to provide more opportunities for regionally based communicators, having started to diversify geographically a decade or so ago. This also reflects the relatively high proportion of locally based communicators in the public sector, including those working in councils, the NHS, police forces, and so on.

However, for a large number of practitioners, especially those who do not necessarily have their roots in London, once they have established their internal communication careers and in an effort to forge a more equitable balance between career and home life, there is an increasingly irresistible pull to move back home, to return to their original communities. Cost of living, commuting times, pressure on personal development time, and long working hours lead many to reevaluate their work–life balance, irrespective of where they originally came from, which says a lot about the demands of the job.

IB: How have you had to adapt to cater for this?

DB: VMA Group launched VMA North in January 2007. Based out of Manchester, our northern office covers a large geographical area, encompassing the whole of the north of England, the north Midlands and Scotland. Our northern offering was launched with an eye-catching, slightly edgy "Tired of London" campaign. The rationale behind the campaign was to acknowledge a growing trend and attract candidates who wanted to get back to their roots in the north or who wanted to move out of London for a better quality and different pace of life. It has certainly struck a chord.

We wanted to educate the communication community in London and the south that there is a strong job market in the north and moving would not be detrimental to continuing a successful communications career. We wanted to change the perception of the north and the business community that exists there. We're pleased to say that we've been pushing against an open door.

Our launch event focused on the northwest and attracted more interest than we ever imagined. We expect that subsequent events covering the Midlands and Scotland will no doubt have similar results. With a number of case studies, including leading communications employers at AstraZeneca and Littlewoods Shop Direct, as well as a number of candidates who had made the transition from south to north, we received some interesting feedback from those who attended. There is a growing realization among many that careers outside London offer an impressive range of employers, a substantially improved quality of life, the potential to maintain salary levels, and, perhaps most enlightening, the opportunity to push a career further and faster outside the capital due to far less competition.

IB: Have you detected any patterns in the impact that issues like employer brand, ethics or values have on choice of employer or employee?

DB: Around a decade ago, I can honestly say that, whatever candidates were thinking, this never really raised its head. Despite the long-standing talk about the war for talent, employers didn't emphasize what many see as the softer aspects of their employment brand. Now, jobseekers in particular increasingly take into account the nature of the business in which they work when seeking a new role. I would say it's an issue in at least 50 percent of the positions we handle.

Whereas international roles in the past may have commanded more interest, with the opportunity to travel and broaden horizons, for many today, roles with global remits do not always sit comfortably with personal values. Issues like "carbon footprint" and wider environmental impacts are increasingly voiced as concerns for today's jobseeker but, most immediately, potential employees are less likely to sacrifice family values for the draw of a glamorous international role. There appears to be less naivety around, in this respect, which means a flashy title, package or brand isn't enough to close a deal.

IB: I don't expect you to point the finger at brands but what industries are appearing on the candidate black list?

DB: Bearing in mind that internal communication professionals have to represent the thoughts, feelings and values of both their employers and employees, they have traditionally been careful about the brands they choose to represent. Certain industries have always been controversial – many communicators used to baulk at the thought of working for a tobacco company, or the arms industry, more so today. But whereas in the past, many would put ethics to one side in their goal of working for major, international corporates offering substantial inducements, increasingly, those corporates who find themselves in sectors perceived as "controversial" are finding it all the more difficult to recruit. These sectors aren't always as obvious as tobacco firms; a number of industries have employment image problems, usually linked to high-profile stories about the way they treat staff, the environment, and customers.

IB: I'm aware that the recent off-shoring and outsourcing of customer service functions, for example, has had a significant negative impact on certain industries which were previously seen as employers of choice. But in your view, how big an impact is the broader work–life balance debate having on the recruitment market?

DB: Corporates are more attuned to the fact that candidates are demanding more work–life balance, the opportunity to work from home, objectives-based performance management rather than clock watching, and flexible working hours to fit in with family life. Few companies tend to offer this flexibility at the outset, and are loathe to set what they see as dangerous precedents so they are unresponsive to pragmatic suggestions. This has undoubtedly led to an increasing demand among many candidates to seek alternative means to achieve a better balance. It seems a short-sighted strategy of many HR directors.

Filling the gap between demand and supply, one of the largest growth areas within the internal communications profession has, interestingly, been the rise of the interim manager. Being a career interim has enabled many practitioners to take control of when and where they work, how much of themselves they devote to the role, and in what capacity. It has given many the opportunity to be part of a team yet without getting involved in the politics (if that isn't a contradiction in itself). Interim management, in particular, lends itself well to the project nature of certain aspects of internal communications, so within the industry, certain individuals are well placed to support those who ultimately want to achieve the work–life balance they aspire to.

Candidates naturally have different motivators but particularly in today's market, where the number of opportunities has outstripped the number of high-calibre candidates, today's jobseeker can and increasingly does demand a working environment that sits far better with their own personal circumstances and values.

RETENTION ISSUES?

David's comments have been echoed by the majority of recruitment professionals I've worked with in the recent past. In some respects, his observations are heartening and emphasize the steady development of the internal communication profession. In many other respects, David's reflections are somewhat disconcerting for employers and equally worrying for the employee engagement community.

The reluctance to develop flexible working practices more in tune with the values of the best candidates bodes particularly ill, as does the growing trend toward interim working. The latter threatens to push the profession back down the engagement staircase with a resounding thump and will doubtless have implications for the brand as short-term focus takes priority over ongoing culture development and the creation of an internal engagement coalition between the communication, marketing, HR and organization development functions.

What this highlights is a significant mismatch between the employer brand that the organization is attempting to develop and the employee brand, namely, what the best candidates actually need. I would encourage employers, be they HR professionals or not, to develop answers to the following:

- What is wrong with the elements that make up your employer brand when you can attract interim communication professionals and yet the same individuals are unwilling to commit to fully employed status?
- Why are your internal communication professionals most valued for their ability to project manage communication, when the job should primarily be concerned with changing behaviors, creating the conditions for truly engaging people rather than pushing messages?

- Why do advertisements for employee engagement specialists ask for HR qualifications, when employee engagement is the pinnacle of the internal communication profession, not an add-on to programmatic HR?
- What do you think the impact on the business will be if you're unable to attract and effectively engage with the leaders who are responsible for coordinating employee engagement?

We've invested significant time talking about the role of chief engagement officers throughout business. But they alone can't guard against the authenticity gap. Internal communication professionals will play an increasingly important part in role modeling, facilitating, and spearheading effective engagement practice. In the story that follows, we hear from a professional working in tandem with her communication community to support the evolution of their brand, a story that has seen one organization travel full circle and return to its values-based roots.

Case Study
VALUES-BASED COMMUNICATION: THE STORY OF THE YORKSHIRE BUILDING SOCIETY: A TRUE MUTUAL

In 19th-century England, the Industrial Revolution erupted into massive social change and, as a by-product of the drive for prosperity, it threatened to tear village communities apart as generations headed into towns and cities to service heavy industry. Building societies emerged as financial mutual help organizations for workers who had been uprooted from their village communities. They offered a way for workers to pool resources and fund and build their own housing in the difficult, often scandalous economic conditions of the new cities. The Yorkshire Building Society (YBS) can trace its roots back to the establishment of the Huddersfield Equitable in 1864 and still remains proudly mutual today. That's quite a brand heritage. But it does have its limitations.

Being a mutual building society means that, unlike most financial services organizations, the Society is run for the benefit of its members rather than for the benefit of shareholders. In addition to the higher savings rates and lower mortgage rates which this implies, the values associated with mutuality run through every facet of the YBS brand. They drive a way of operating an internal culture and a business philosophy which look very different from those seen in non-mutual financial service organizations.

The Society's purpose: "To maximize long-term benefits for a growing membership" neatly summarizes this distinctive position. It is reflected in an internal culture that blends a long view – traditional ethics with modern business efficiency. It places a premium on building personal relationships and collaborative working, and embodies a warmth, sincerity, and intimacy that are uncommon in financial services. You only have to visit its welcoming headquarters to feel this intimacy. But markets change and in an industry where analysts view performance in quarterly bursts and customers and employers are driving the consumer economy at a rapid pace, the mutuals began to look outdated.

In the 1980s, like many financial services organizations at the time, YBS experimented with diversification into areas such as estate agency and direct provision of financial planning advice.

Having had its metaphorical fingers burnt, a far more cautious approach emerged during the 1990s and persisted into the first half of the 2000s. During this period, the Yorkshire Building Society returned to its core competence, concentrating on mainstream savings and mortgage products and playing only in its traditional, risk-averse prime retail markets. While other lenders entered emerging markets such as the increasingly profitable buy-to-let sector and started to build a sales culture, the YBS continued to concentrate on its mainstream product range and providing exceptional customer service through exemplary employees.

By 2004, however, YBS received a real call to adventure, as it had become apparent that, despite the efforts of its leaders, this was not a sustainable long-term strategy. The whole sector was experiencing significant pressure on margins and the cautious approach adopted by the Society was resulting in single-digit growth figures rather than the 14–15 percent growth being achieved by other banks and building societies. A number of mutuals surrendered their status, believing that their brands and operating principles would allow them to compete with the independents. The market, no longer tied by the same needs or always respecting the same values as the original customer base of the mutuals, demanded more.

Emma Snyder, internal communication manager takes up the story.

It became clear to our leaders that a new approach was needed at the YBS. We needed to unfreeze the culture a little to allow a little change in. "Step Change" was the name given to this new approach which called for more risk taking, entry to new markets and a greater emphasis upon optimizing the existing relationship with customers. Crucially, every time this was communicated to employees, it carried a significant rider – all this had to be achieved within the framework of the existing values of the organization.

It was widely understood that this meant not just the published formal values of fun, fairness, passion and people working together, but also the unspoken, traditional values of the Yorkshire Building Society, which stemmed from our geography and founding philosophy. For those people who don't know Yorkshire, let's just say that it's populated by friendly but forthright, pragmatic, stoic people, but is a diverse, vibrant county with a growing sense of self-confidence. This proved critical. While acknowledging the need for a new approach, the leadership of the Society had observed the impact of short-term decision making, the disturbing omens, unbridled dominance of sales targets, and the disregard for fairness and service to customers in some of the other banks and building societies who were clearly becoming more detached from their customer base. The YBS leaders were, and remain, absolutely determined to avoid these outcomes at the Yorkshire.

Step Change deliberately impacted the branch network the most quickly and substantially. Branch staff were consulted and involved in the development of a new sales framework and product range. Branch staff also received extensive training to proactively identify customers' needs and to offer products to meet those needs. At any other organization, you might be justified in seeing in this the beginnings of a soulless sales culture, but at the Yorkshire it is genuinely positioned as part of providing exceptional customer service in an authentic way, in tune with the values. The premium that the Society places on building personal relationships, the absolute essence of the Yorkshire brand, has survived the impact of Step Change in the branch network untarnished and in fact greatly strengthened.

Unlike most branch staff in financial services, YBS branch staff do not wear uniforms to set them apart from customers. Branches are laid out to allow maximum interaction between staff and customers. Comfortable seating areas, children's toys, and coffee machines are provided for customers' use. The brand livery reflected in all communication is bright and engaging. The whole feel is very welcoming, very personal, very relaxed, and very Yorkshire and this is echoed in the non-customer facing units.

One of the most significant changes has been in the Society's approach to internal communication and staff engagement. Back in 2004, with a recent history of limited and mainly evolutionary change, the Society's attitude toward formal internal communication and engagement was typical of a small, traditional company with a broadly paternalistic approach to its staff. In other words, internal communication was fairly haphazard, flowed down through the hierarchy, and epitomized the model of "we'll tell you what's going on when we think you need to know (and if we remember)." It wasn't a control issue but more of a fact that the leadership felt they should own and manage communication to ensure that employees had the information they needed and weren't troubled by too much of it. They were old-fashioned threshold guardians.

To cater for more formal communication, a single writer was attached to the marketing department and was responsible for producing a quarterly newspaper. It was more of a gesture than anything. The marketing area, believing that there really ought to be some value in internal communication, was keen to hang onto the function, but was unsure where and how to drive out that value and struggled to give it the profile it needed.

Prompted by the introduction of Step Change, senior members of the HR team identified that employees really needed to be engaged with the change process relating to the YBS brand more effectively and that this required a more professional approach to internal communication. They appreciated that a decision means nothing until it has been communicated in a way that inspires action. As part of a more strategic approach to all aspects of organization development, they undertook a strategic review of all people policies, including learning and development, internal communication and engagement. The feedback was overwhelmingly in favor of more effective communication, this became the basis of the business case and, as a result, a new internal communication (IC) team was recruited and established within the HR department.

The brief for the new team was to join up internal communication and engagement with the strategic goals of the organization and in particular to help to move from an information-push model to a more engagement-led model. In fact *engaging people* is just one of a new set of leadership competencies recently introduced.

Early, significant, and high-profile wins have included the design of a recent interactive management conference with the theme of inspirational leadership; a joint effort between the IC team, the learning and development team, and the PR team – the value of "people working together" in action.

Some other successes of the internal communication team include:

- The fact that employee engagement is now regarded as a strategic activity. The team has a voice at the senior level, sees itself as working in partnership with managers and is acknowledged as having a significant degree of influence in the organization
- Formal communication planning has been introduced, with a small set of defined key messages and a rolling 12-month plan, which is updated monthly and shared with all senior managers who provide feedback
- Great value is placed upon personal relationships and this translates into a focus on enabling local managers to communicate themselves rather than creating swathes of glossy, centrally developed materials
- A much stronger emphasis has been placed on explaining the context, reasons, and background for decisions in communications
- Internal communication is now regarded as integral and fundamental to all project and initiative launches and the IC team is routinely involved at the formative planning stages rather than sweeping up at the end
- The "Pipeline" has replaced a number of email, paper and word-of-mouth communication methods by bringing together all operational-type messaging into one intranet-based channel. A community of business authors and editors is in place who craft messages to a familiar format based on the principles of information mapping. Messages appear twice daily and are streamed by audience, radically reducing the amount of communication clutter
- Other new communication channels have been introduced such as a quarterly magazine, managers' briefing packs, a staff message board, listening groups, monthly core brief, leadership workshops, and management conferences. Many of these channels incorporate a strong emphasis upon two-way communication and have been modeled on the core values

- The general management team has been given a much higher profile in the organization and is now more visible and accessible
- There is a major new project to replace the majority of the content on the sprawling legacy intranet with a collaborative knowledge management solution. Implementation of this solution is ongoing
- A quarterly staff opinion survey has been introduced, which will include organizational KPIs for leadership, culture, satisfaction, and engagement, raising the prominence and focus on these strategic objectives to board level. It will also deliver much more frequent and targeted feedback to local leaders than a traditional, weighty, biannual staff opinion survey
- A recognition scheme for HO staff has been launched, incorporating peer nominations and local awarding.

Today, the Yorkshire is proud to operate 134, value-adding branches in an industry that has gone call center crazy, and we pride ourselves on personable customer service in an industry where process has replaced passion. The Yorkshire advertises on TV much less frequently than other banks and building societies and has only a tiny budget for direct mail because it believes the brand is all about the individual, warm relationships built at a local level with customers.

The Society is achieving double-digit year-on-year growth while simultaneously reducing costs – a record any plc would envy. There is a discernible new dynamism around the place, an energy and focus that had waned in the light of changes within its market just a few years before. Step Change has done its work and continues to drive change but the Society has achieved this success without compromising the warm, intimate, relationship-based culture and its founding principles. The empire building and politics seen in many large plcs are notable by their absence. Managers talk about developing stronger emotional connections with their staff, understanding them better, helping them to develop. The scores achieved in the quarterly staff opinion survey support the perception that there has been a huge improvement in this area. For example, to the question: "Considering everything, I am satisfied with YBS as an employer," the score was 89 percent affirmative in the 2007 pilot versus 74 percent in the 2005 survey.

Branch staff talk about understanding their customers better, meeting their needs, delivering an exceptional level of service. Mystery shopping and customer satisfaction scores consistently over 90 percent indicate this is working and that the YBS brand is thriving. These hard facts are backed up by everyday legends of customer service like the middle manager who works in Bradford head office and who recently hand delivered a set of deeds to a customer in Edinburgh or the branch manager who recently ran a mile from his branch to a mortgage customer's dental practice to get a document signed so that a house completion could take place on time. Rare tales in an industry languishing under a gray cloud of customer criticism.

They may not be a global brand but the YBS team has set itself an ambitious future challenge:

> We want our customers to see the Society as one of the best organizations, of any type, that they do business with.

The internal communication team sees its role in supporting this goal as, quite simply, helping the Society to become better at communicating and connecting with itself to bring the brand to life. Some of the key IC initiatives that will support this are:

- embedding a collaborative approach to knowledge management, which involves all staff
- a collaborative project with the branch network to review and maximize the performance of their channel set
- the redesign of their monthly core briefing process in conjunction with people managers from around the business
- a three-level program of communication skills training, which will range from sharing specialized communication techniques such as storytelling with senior managers through to back to basics writing skills
- the roll-out and support of the quarterly staff opinion surveys
- the gradual launch of social media-type channels such as blogs and wikis
- a collaborative project with HR to look at the communication processes around recruitment and induction.

Speaking for Emma, the YBS internal communication team is not the only hero in this journey. What this case study seeks to demonstrate is that the approach taken to internal communication in any organization needs to be synchronized 100 percent with its strategic goals and its value set. The Yorkshire Building Society is an organization that respects the origins of its market, its own history, its business philosophy, and the way it goes about things. This story of the professionalization of internal communication within YBS is a story rooted firmly within this social context. It is really a reflection in microcosm of the story of the development of the brand itself, and the values the society projects certainly appear to resonate with these changing times. The YBS was faced with becoming a legacy brand; out of time; a relic. It now has another chance to build on its heritage and start to work toward a more proactive story more befitting the age.

YBS may not be a multinational plc but there's a great deal many plcs can take from this modest tale.

IN CONCLUSION

I began this journey with a quote about starting a revolution. I asserted that we should "burn the effigy of brand alignment" as it's a term which epitomizes the reactionary attitude toward brand development and is the anathema of employee engagement.

But, as this particular journey reaches its conclusion, I'm reminded of the character, Granger from Ray Bradbury's apocalyptic, book-burning epic, *Fahrenheit 451* who laments the fact that, even when they weren't hunting down and burning books, they weren't using the lore within them.

With this image plucking at our collective conscience I'm very conscious that the legacy this particular offering will leave will largely depend on the impact the observations, reflections, methodologies, and shared stories, modestly proffered, will have on readers.

The challenge goes out, therefore, to brand managers and ceos alike to break from the pack and start to look beyond the physical manifestations of their brand, to extend their ambition beyond current brand valuation metrics and begin to recognize the secret of authentic brand development. By embracing the notion that sustainable brand development stems from employees who are truly engaged with the business you'll be on the start of the journey toward fulfilling the potential of your brand.

As we've illustrated, effective brand engagement doesn't come in a single package. It involves:

- the development of a clear business case focused on the values, goals, and objectives of the business as well as the legacy the leaders want to leave
- the creation of an internal brand management alliance between the custodians of internal communication

- the acknowledgement that chief engagement officers don't sit at the top but are required at all levels in the business
- a clear and inclusive brand development and engagement strategy
- a clear understanding of current and desired future culture and a plan to move between the two
- stimulating, capturing and sharing the story as it emerges.

I've very much enjoyed the process of gathering together the thoughts, reflections, and contributions that have made this extended tale possible and while I hope you, in turn, have enjoyed the journey, I sincerely hope that the odd flash of inspiration will have lit a fuse or two along the way.

At the beginning, I made the ambitious assertion that brand management can have a profound impact on the things that matter most to our society by helping us refocus our collective consciousness back onto the things that really matter. You can tell a lot about what society values by the relationship between the structures that dominate our mental and our physical landscapes, the places where brands literally shine brightest. I can't help thinking that we've missed the point somewhat in recent times. As trees and mountains have been replaced by megaliths and totems, village halls by churches, churches by castles, castles by palaces, palaces by corporate HQs, spirituality by corporate policy and corporate HQs by corporate brands and the World Wide Web, we've lost the connections and something has fallen through the cracks at each successive stage, something's missing.

Part of the joy of working within the communication business is that it's omnipresent and is, therefore, always evolving. It's the mystery of not knowing what lies around the corner that makes the profession so engaging in its own right. But if there's a chance that internal communicators can contribute toward the process of addressing some of the major issues affecting our corporate culture (and even beyond), there's at least an opportunity for a heroic ending.

The challenge extends to all of us to recognize the power of great communication, its influence on our brands, and to seek out and support local chief engagement officers. It's high time there was a passionate movement to unite value sets in the interest of making our businesses more effective and our time working together more fulfilling. We can achieve this by developing competence across the engagement continuum and by developing a joined-up approach to brand management, which creates authentic brands in tune with the changing times. We can improve the cultures we live in by improving the performance of the brands that support the full range of our needs, even if it means being brave enough to open the doors to alternative ways of seeing and encouraging our colleagues and peers to really bring themselves to work.

With this in mind, I ask you to indulge me one last time. Whether you're a captain of industry or a poet, a team leader or a self-employed, one-man band, please take a moment to pause and allow yourself to reflect on your own chief engagement role. Now consider how you're going to return to your own particular community, the fresh insights you're going to bring, and how you're going to engage the people you care about to embrace a small handful of alternative ways.

What will be my legacy?

In this role
In my career
At home
On this planet
What three things will I do differently?
Tomorrow
By next month
By next year

Good luck and please do stop by from time to time and let me know how you get on.

Ian
www.by2w.co.uk

POSTSCRIPT

I use the journey metaphor a great deal in my work and throughout this book. The creative and production process has been an exhilarating journey in its own right. As with all epics, it has not been without its challenges which have called upon reserves of collaboration and compromise.

As authenticity is one of the cornerstones of this book, I feel obliged to point out that an important compromise for me has been the decision to allow the work to be published in US English.

I trust that this decision will be seen for what it is – a recognition that the largest part of the market globally apparently will be most familiar with US English. But you, the customer, have the final say so if you do have a view on this increasing trend or indeed have any other feedback, I very much encourage you to make your views known. I look forward to hearing what you think.

BIBLIOGRAPHY

Colyer E. (2003) *Promoting Brand Allegiance Within*, www.brandchannel.com

Prologue

Buckingham, Ian (2005) *Survey of chief engagement officers*, Bring Yourself 2 Work

Mumford, Chris (2007) Older and wiser, *Insight* (www.hotelreport.co.uk and www.hospitalitynet.org), which quoted the Egremont Research conducted by YouGov plc for RightNow Technologies and which was quoted in the *Sunday Times*, February 2007

Smith, David (2007) quotes Jonathon Porritt, Stop shopping or the planet will go pop, *Observer*, 8 April 2007 and quotes in *The Ecologist* online, 10 April 2007, www.theecologist.org.

Smythe Dorward Lambert (2000) *Internal Communication Survey*, 2000

Wilde, Oscar, *Michael Moncur's Cynical Quotations*, www.quotationspage.com

Woodward, Clive (2005) *Winning*, London, Hodder and Stoughton

Act 1

Bennis, Warren (1997) quoted in Buckingham, Ian and Kitchen, Phillip (2005) Who is responsible for corporate communications?, *Admap,* July/August

Blake, William (1982) *Selected Poems,* London, JM Dent and Sons

Buckingham, Ian (2005) *Survey of chief engagement officers*, Bring Yourself 2 Work

Buckingham, Ian and Kitchen, Phillip (2005) Who is responsible for corporate communications?, *Admap,* July/August

Fombrun, Charles (1996) quoted in Buckingham, Ian and Kitchen, Phillip (2005) Who is responsible for corporate communications?, *Admap*, July/August

George, William W. (2007) *True North: Discover Your Authentic Leadership*, New York, Jossey-Bass (*The Wall Street Journal* Best Seller List)

Leahy, Terry (2007) quote from *How Green is Your High Street?*, BBC2, June

Lucier, Chuck , Spiegel, Eric and Schuyt, Rob (2002) *Why CEOs Fall: The Causes and Consequences of Turnover at the Top*, Booz Allen Hamilton

Melcrum (2005) *Employee Engagement,* March, http://www.melcrum.com/store/products/product.shtml?id=2401

Milligan, Andy and Smith, Shaun (eds) (2002) *Uncommon Practice,* Harlow, Pearson Education. Extracts reproduced with permission

Mumford, Chris (2007) Older and wiser, *Insight* (www.hotelreport.co.uk and www.hospitalitynet.org), which quoted the Egremont Research conducted by YouGov plc for RightNow Technologies and which was quoted in the *Sunday Times,* February 2007

Orwell, George (1983) *Keep the Aspidistra Flying,* London, Penguin

Pine, B. Joseph II and Gilmour, James H. (1999) *The Experience Economy: Work Is Theatre and Every Business a Stage,* Boston, Harvard Business School Press

Pringle, Hamish and Gordon, William (2001) *Brand Manners,* Chichester, Wiley. Copyright John Wiley & Sons Ltd. Reproduced with permission

Sykes, J. B. (ed.) (1986) *The Concise Oxford Dictionary,* London, Guild Publishing

Act 2

Austin, Jonathan (2007) *The Sunday Times Best 100 Companies to Work For Survey, Times* supplement

Campbell, Joseph (2001) *The Power of Myth,* New York, Broadway Books

Day, Anthony (2007) Going Green: Inspiring People, seminar run by MotivAction and held in London's Commonwealth Club, June

Gilliam, Terry (1985) *Brazil,* Universal Studios, 20th Century Fox

Handy, Charles (1997) *The Hungry Spirit,* London, Hutchinson

Khilnani, Sunil (2003) *The Idea of India,* London, Penguin

Kubrick, Stanley (1968) *2001: A Space Odyssey,* Warner Brothers

Lott, Tim (2007) *The New Middle Classes,* BBC4, June

Michaelis, Peter (2007) *Consumers' Concerns about Climate Change,* Norwich Union Ethical Research, www.aviva.com

Morgan, Gareth (1989) *Creative Organization Theory,* USA, Sage

Organic Farmers & Growers (2004) *National Benchmark Survey of Organic Food Production*

Soil Association (2004) *Organic Food and Farming Report*

Suchman, Lucy (2007) Anthropology as Brand, paper presented at the Colloquium on Interdisciplinarity and Society, Oxford University, February 24

YouGov (2006) A Measure of Melancholy, poll Commissioned by the *Sunday Times,* www.yougov.com

Act 3

Austin, Jonathan (2007) *The Sunday Times Best 100 Companies to Work For Survey*, *Times* supplement

Bernoulli's principle, *Wikipedia*, www.wikipedia.org

Buckingham, Ian (2007) Want better DM yields? Ask your internal comms department, *Argent*, winter

Carroll, Lewis (1998) *Through the Looking-Glass and What Alice Found There*, London, Macmillan Children's Books

Fisher-McGarry, Julie (2006) *Be the Change You Want to See in the World*, Conari Press

Huba, Jackie and McConnell, Ben (2006) *Citizen Marketers: When People are The Message*, New York, Kaplan Business

Melcrum, *Employee Engagement*, March 2005, http://www.melcrum.com/store/products/product.shtml?id=2401

Melcrum (2006) Essential data on budgets, salaries and trends, *The Pulse*, October, http://www.melcrum.com/store/products/product.shtml?id=3256

Office of National Statistics (2001) *Census of Faiths or Belief Systems*

Pringle, Hamish and Gordon, William (2001) *Brand Manners*, Chichester, Wiley. Copyright John Wiley & Sons Ltd. Reproduced with permission

Quirke, Bill (2000) *Making the Connections: Using Internal Communication to Turn Strategy into Action*, Hampshire, Gower (new edition due 2008)

Act 4

Human Synergistics International (2003) *Organizational Culture Inventory Interpretation & Development Guide*, Plymouth, MI, USA.

Act 5

Buckingham, Ian (2005) *Survey of chief engagement officers*, Bring Yourself 2 Work

Byham, William C. with Cox, Jeff (1991) *ZAPP!: The Lightning of Empowerment*, Chatham, Century Business

Campbell, Joseph (2001) *The Power of Myth*, New York, Broadway Books. Extracts reproduced with permission

Coelho, Paul (1999) *The Alchemist*, San Francisco, HarperCollins

Gilliam, Terry (1985) *Brazil*, Universal Studios, 20th Century Fox

Gray, John (2002) *Men are from Mars, Women are from Venus*, London, HarperCollins

Johnson, Spencer (1998) *Who Moved My Cheese?*, London, Vermillion

Milligan, Andy and Smith, Shaun (eds) (2002) *Uncommon Practice*, Harlow, Pearson Education. Extracts reproduced with permission

Shakespeare, William *Hamlet, Prince of Denmark*, Thompson, A. and Taylor, N. (eds) (2006) The Arden Shakespeare (3rd series), London, Thompson Learning

A Selection of Related Further Reading

Appleyard, Bryan (2007) Because we're worth it, *Sunday Times* magazine, May 27

Atkinson, Philip E. (1990) *Creating Culture Change: The Key to Successful Total Quality Management*, London, IFS Ltd

Barthes, Roland (1977) *Image–Music–Text*, London, Fontana

Belasco, James A. and Stayer, Ralph C. (1993) *Flight of the Buffalo Soaring to Excellence: Learning to Let Employees Lead*, New York, Warner Books

Bianco, Anthony and Lavelle, Louis (2000) The CEO trap, *BusinessWeek*, December 11, www.businessweek.com

Blanchard, Kenneth, Carew, Donald and Parisi-Carew, Eunice (1992) *The One Minute Manager Builds High Performing Teams*, London, HarperCollins

Bloom, Michael (2002) *Thinking Like a Director*, London, Faber & Faber

Booker, Christopher (2005) *The Seven Basic Plots: Why We Tell Stories*, London, Continuum International Publishing Group

Braid, Mary (2007) How to hold onto footloose graduates, *Sunday Times*, July 15

Braid, Mary (2007) How to connect with generation Y, *Sunday Times*, May 20

Broadbent, Tim (2000) *Advertising Works II*, London, NTC Publications

Buckingham, Ian (2005) Culture as a competitive weapon, *Admap*, March

Buckingham, Ian (2006) Innovation or inertia? The eternal dilemma, *Admap*, summer

Buckingham, Ian and Roberts, John (2006) Is yours a "flagging" brand? *Admap*, May

Buckingham, Ian and Miller, Paul (2007) Becoming an "authentic" business, *Personnel Today*, June

Campbell, Joseph (1992) *The Masks of God: Primitive Mythology*, Vol. 1, New York, Arkana (New Ed edition)

Campbell, Joseph (2003) *The Hero's Journey: Joseph Campbell on his Life and Work*, New York, New World Library (Ed edition)

Campbell, Joseph (2004) *Pathways to Bliss: Mythology and Personal Transformation*, New York, New World Library

Cockman, Peter, Evans, Bill and Reynolds, Peter (1992) *Client-centred Consulting*, Maidenhead, McGraw-Hill

Collins, Jim (2001) *Good to Great*, New York, Random House

Covey, Steven R. (1998) *The 7 Habits of Highly Effective People*, New York, Simon & Schuster

George, William W. (2003) Authentic leaders: devote yourself to a cause, *Executive Excellence*, October

George, William W. (2003) Authentic leaders needed to restore trust, *Minneapolis Star Tribune*, December 15

George, William W. (2004) Find your voice, *Harvard Business Review*, **82**(1): 35

George, William W. (2004) Meditate on it, *Harvard Business Review*, **82**(1)

George, William W. (2004) The journey to authenticity, *Leader to Leader*, **31**, winter

George, William W. (2004) Values drive performance, *Executive Excellence*, March

George, William W. (2004) Waking up a sleeping company, *HBS Working Knowledge*, April 12

George, William W. (2006) The master gives it back, *U.S. News & World Report*, October 30: 66–8

George, William W. (2006) Truly authentic leadership, *U.S. News & World Report*, October 30: 52–4

George, William W. and McLean, Andrew N. (2007) Why leaders lose their way, *Strategy and Leadership*, **35**(3)

George, William W., Sims, Peter, McLean, Andrew N. and Mayer, Diana (2007) Discovering your authentic leadership, *Harvard Business Review*, **85**(2)

Giuliani, Rudolph W. (2002) *Leadership*, London, Hyperion

Godin, Seth (2005) *All Marketers are Liars*, New York, Portfolio

Greene, Robert (2006) *The 33 Strategies of War,* London, Profile Books

Hamel, Gary (2000) *Leading The Revolution*, Boston, HBS Press

Jensen Group, The (1998) *Changing the Way We Work: The Search for a Simpler Way*, London: The Jensen Group

Kitchen, Philip and Schultz, Don (2001) *Raising the Corporate Umbrella*, Basingstoke, Macmillan – now Palgrave Macmillan

Knight, Sue (2001) *NLP at Work*, London, Nicholas Brealey Publishing

Kuczmarski, Susan Smith, and Kuczmarski, Thomas D. (1995) *Values-based Leadership*, New Jersey, Prentice Hall

Lansberg, Ivan (1999) *Succeeding Generations*, Boston, HBS Press

Maister, David H. (1997) *Managing the Professional Service Firm*, London, Free Press

Maister, David H. (2001) *Practice What You Preach*, London, Free Press

Mendels, Pamela (2002) The real cost of firing a CEO, *Chief Executive*, April, www.chiefexecutive.net/depts/corpgov/177.htm

Mitter, Shomit (1992) *Systems of Rehearsal*, London, Routledge

Nordstrom, Kjell and Ridderstrale, Jonas (2001) *Funky Business*, New Jersey, Prentice Hall

Nordstrom, Kjell and Ridderstrale, Jonas (2004) *Karaoke Capitalism: Managing for Mankind*, New Jersey, Prentice Hall

Pearce, Terry (2003) *Leading Out Loud*, San Francisco, Jossey-Bass

Schultz, Don and Walters, Jeffery (1997) *Measuring Brand Communication ROI*, Association of National Advertisers

Simmons, John (2003) *The Invisible Grail: In Search of the True Language of Brands*, London, Texere

Stern, Stefan (2007) Why managers need to engage with grumpy employees, FT.com, May 15

ten Have, Steven, ten Have, Wouter, Stevens, Frans and van der Elst, Marcel (2003) *Key Management Models*, Harlow, Pearson

INDEX

D

Darumas 159
Data 116, 124
Davis, Miles 7
Day, Anthony 39
Deficiency needs 48
Deloitte 39
Demographic 129, 131
Department of Health 100
Depersonalized 38
Design 5, 53, 111
Design houses 53
Development process 45
Diagnostic 120–1
Diary room 120
Direct mail 93–4
Diversity 47, 59–62, 72, 77, 137
DNA 67, 76, 119, 143, 187
Dreams 91
Ducks in a row 124

E

Eco-friendly 39
Eco-warriors 113
Ecological 56
Effeminate 51
Emasculated 187
Emotion/al 12–14, 28, 41, 45, 47,
   54, 114, 136, 186
Empathy 54, 126, 137, 145, 169, 179
Emperor's new clothes 15
Employee
   Attitude 6–7
   Brand 54, 100, 172
   Consultation 23, 108
   Engagement 8, 11–13, 15, 21,
      24–6 (drivers of), 27, 45, 53,
      58, 74, 83, 114, 128, 137,
      170–4, 182, 193
   Involvement 59
   Perspective 49, 91–2
   Relations 105

Retention 133
Satisfaction 52, 177
Surveys 122
Turnover 6, 188
Employer
   Brand 26, 150, 191–3
   of Choice 150, 185
Employment brand 35, 92, 112, 144,
   188
Empowerment 27, 37, 56
Endings (comic, heroic, tragic)
   164–6
Energy centers 141
Energy investment indicator 141
Energy Saving Trust (EST) 40
Engage (engagement, engaging) 21,
   48, 83, 104, 120, 124, 151,
   164–6, 170
Engagement
   Continuum 121, 174
   Drivers 113
   Events 128
   Filter 49
   Interventions 121
   Process 114, 122, 178
   Program 54–5
   Staircase 99, 143
   Strategy 84, 175
England gymnastics 185
England rugby 7
English 62
Enron 27, 141
Environment/al 22, 39, 48, 56
Ernst and Young 39
Epic 164
Esteem 56
Ethics 22, 40, 191–2
European Institute for Managing
   Diversity 137
Events 51, 131
Everyman 9, 11, 46, 81, 135, 162
Existentialism 37
Experience economy 184
Experiences 11–13, 34, 78